PENGUIN CLASSICS

THE JUGURTHINE WAR
THE CONSPIRACY OF CATILINE

ADVISORY EDITOR: BETTY RADICE

GAIUS SALLUSTIUS CRISPUS (86 – c. 35 B.C.) was born in the Sabine highlands of central Italy. In his youth an active supporter of the anti-senatorial party, Sallust became a quaestor and, in 52, a tribune of the plebs. In the year 50 he was expelled from the Senate for alleged immorality, but a year or so later the influence of Julius Caesar enabled him to be re-elected and to re-enter the Senate. He was Caesar's officer in various campaigns of the civil war from 49 to 45, and was installed by him as governor of Numidia. Sallust is said to have enriched himself so blatantly at the expense of the province that he was only saved from condemnation by Caesar's protection (possibly secured by an enormous bribe). He became extremely wealthy, owning a villa at Tivoli said to have been Caesar's, and a mansion and lovely park at Rome, the famous *horti Sallustiani*, later the property of the Roman Emperors.

After Caesar's death he retired from public life and spent the rest of his life in literary composition, for which he was probably much better suited. His two surviving works, the monographs on the conspiracy of Catiline and the Jugurthine war, written between 44 and 40 B.C., were much admired in the antique world. Sallust also wrote *A History of Rome* in five books, covering the period from Sulla's death in 78 to the year 67, but only fragments of this survive.

S. A. HANDFORD was born at Manchester in 1898 and educated at Bradford Grammar School and at Balliol College, Oxford, where he took a 'double first' in classics. He was a lecturer in Swansea, and Lecturer and Reader at King's College, London. He published several books on classical subjects, and translated Caesar, Sallust and Aesop for the Penguin Classics. He died in October 1978.

SALLUST

THE JUGURTHINE WAR

THE CONSPIRACY OF CATILINE

TRANSLATED WITH AN INTRODUCTION
BY S. A. HANDFORD

PENGUIN BOOKS

Penguin Books Ltd, Harmondsworth, Middlesex, England
Viking Penguin Inc., 40 West 23rd Street, New York, New York 10010, U.S.A.
Penguin Books Australia Ltd, Ringwood, Victoria, Australia
Penguin Books Canada Limited, 2801 John Street, Markham, Ontario, Canada L3R 1B4
Penguin Books (N.Z.) Ltd, 182–190 Wairau Road, Auckland 10, New Zealand

—

First published 1963
Reprinted 1967, 1969, 1970, 1972, 1975, 1977, 1979, 1980,
1982, 1983, 1985, 1987

—

—

Printed and bound in Great Britain by
Cox & Wyman Ltd, Reading
Set in Monotype Bembo

CONTENTS

CONTENTS

The Latin texts of the *Bellum Iugurthinum* and the *Catilinae Coniuratio* are divided into sections and subsections, which are indicated by the numbers shown in the page-headings of this translation. These numbers are used in the introductions and footnotes to refer to passages of the translation.

LIFE AND WRITINGS OF SALLUST

THE information we possess about the career of Gaius Sallustius Crispus is meagre, and, in spite of the high moral tone which he adopts in those passages of his works that deal with political and social matters, very little of what is known reflects any credit upon him. He was born in 86 B.C., in the Sabine highlands of central Italy, became a quaestor about 55 and a tribune of the plebs in 52, during which year he tried to secure the condemnation of Milo – a political gang-leader who was on trial for the murder of his rival Clodius – and attacked Cicero for defending Milo. Since Clodius had been a bitter enemy of Cicero and some years earlier had been one of Caesar's chief henchmen, this action marked Sallust as a supporter of the *populares*, the anti-senatorial group of politicians, among whom Caesar – still engaged at the time in the conquest of Gaul – had been since the late sixties one of the most prominent.

In 50 B.C. Sallust was expelled from the Senate by the censors for alleged immorality: no doubt his private life was no more above reproach than that of many of his contemporaries, though much that was said about him by his enemies was mere malicious gossip. A year or two later, however, the influence of Caesar enabled him to be elected to a second quaestorship and so to re-enter the Senate. During the years 49–45 he served Caesar as an officer in various campaigns of the civil war, was elected praetor (46), and was installed by Caesar as proconsular governor of the Province of *Africa Nova*, which had been formed from the kingdom of Juba, king of Numidia. He is said to have plundered the province disgracefully and to have been saved from condemnation only by the protection of Caesar, to whom his enemies said he gave an enormous bribe. Certainly he was thereafter a wealthy man, owning a villa at Tivoli that had been Caesar's and a mansion and a splendid park at Rome – the famous *horti Sallustiani* which afterwards became the property of the Roman emperors. After Caesar's death he retired from public life, for which perhaps he had little real aptitude or taste, and devoted his remaining years to literary composition. He died about 35 B.C.

Sallust's two surviving works – his account of Catiline's conspiracy at Rome in 63 B.C., and his history of the war fought by the Romans with Jugurtha king of Numidia (112–105 B.C.) – were written between the death of Julius Caesar in 44 and the year 40.* In addition to these treatises dealing with episodes that particularly interested him, he wrote a continuous history of the period from Sulla's death in 78 to the year 67; but of this only a few set speeches and letters and a quantity of short narrative fragments survive.

In the absence of this more ambitious work, he can be judged only by his famous monographs. These were much admired throughout classical antiquity, especially by Quintilian and Tacitus, who was directly influenced by them, and later by St Jerome and St Augustine. They continued to be popular through the greater part of the Middle Ages, and were more often laid under contribution by writers of those times, to supply ideas or suggest turns of phrase, than any other pagan author.

All this was a tribute rather to the dramatic qualities of Sallust's narratives, his vivid presentation of the leading characters, and the effectiveness of his literary style, than to his strictly historical merits. In the ancient world, historians were less concerned than they are nowadays with the detailed investigation of facts by means of critical research. They tended to regard history not as the rigorous pursuit of truth with a view to its correct interpretation, but either as a branch of poetry – a sort of prose epic – composed in order to please and to instruct the reader in the traditions of his people or of other peoples, or else as a branch of rhetoric or philosophy, which sought to inspire him by presenting vividly before his eyes the great men and great actions of the past, to impress him by preaching sermons upon the proven consequences of vice and depravity, or finally to enlist his sympathy by attacking or defending the characters and motives of particular groups or individuals. Thus Sallust was not the only historian whose chief interest lay in reconstructing striking

* The *Catiline* was written before the *Jugurthine War*, but in this translation the books are placed in their historical order.

scenes and personages, pathetic or picturesque episodes (even if they were not particularly important), in moralizing about the degeneracy of the present or the recent past, and in putting forward a convincing case for or against those whom he admired or disliked.

Sallust tells us that he chose the theme of Catiline's conspiracy because it was a criminal enterprise of unexampled wickedness and involved Rome in unexampled perils. It was, therefore, an ideal theme for a writer with his special gifts of lively characterization and description, and he took splendid advantage of the opportunities it gave him. Apart from the conventional and rather irrelevant moralizing of the early chapters (many of the sentiments in which are borrowed from various Greek authors), the *Catiline* is a masterpiece of dramatic narrative, marred only by a few inaccuracies of chronology – which must be due to carelessness or indifference, since he was writing of events that happened when he himself was in his early twenties, and for which plenty of material was available – and perhaps by some distortion of fact resulting from a prejudice against Cicero and in favour of Caesar.

In section 5 of the *Jugurthine War* Sallust gives his reasons for selecting it as a subject:

> First, because it was a hard-fought and bloody contest in which victories alternated with defeats; secondly, because it was at this time that the first challenge was offered to the arrogance of the Roman nobles – the beginning of a struggle that played havoc with all our institutions, human and divine, and reached such a pitch of fury that civil strife was ended only by a war which left Italy a desert.

So far as the war itself was concerned, he was attracted mainly by the chances it gave him to write up exciting incidents and to set off against one another the characters of the protagonists – Jugurtha himself, Adherbal, Metellus, Marius, Sulla, and Bocchus. In giving a coherent and properly balanced account of the campaigns he was much less interested, and the historical defects are here more serious than in the *Catiline*. Like some other ancient historians, Sallust had not the technical knowledge – even had he cared enough about the matter – to give lucid and accurate details about siege operations or battle formations; and although he himself lived for some time in

Africa, he often leaves us ill-informed on geographical points such as the position of towns and battlefields and the direction of marches. The chronology gets more confused as the war progresses, because Sallust either did not know or has omitted to tell us in what year certain events occurred. An even more serious fault is that the crucial campaigns of Marius – who was rightly regarded by Sallust as the real victor, the wonder-general raised from the ranks of the *plebs* to save his country in the teeth of senatorial obstruction – are dealt with so sketchily that it is not easy to make out what really happened.*

The second reason put forward by Sallust was probably more important in his eyes. The repeated accusations of treason he makes against the senatorial nobles – to say nothing of the abusive attack upon them that he puts into Marius's mouth – show clearly his bias in favour of the 'popular' side in Roman politics. In Marius there appeared for the first time a man of the people who was such an able soldier and such a powerful personality that he could not be brushed aside: a man who, rising from an obscure origin to be consul, first brought Rome's exhausting struggle with Jugurtha to an end and then went on to repel a far more serious threat from her northern frontier. These events provided Sallust with an excellent opportunity to set the selfish, incompetent, corrupt noblemen against the brilliant plebeian who rescued his country from the dire peril into which they had let it fall. Of course the contrast is overdrawn. Though Sallust is fair to Metellus, the aristocratic commander who was dismissed to make room for Marius, he is certainly less than fair to Scaurus, and his charges of wholesale bribery are certainly exaggerated. No doubt there were dishonest rogues among the nobility, and no doubt money changed hands; but to talk as if Jugurtha regularly kept half the Senate in his pay was ridiculous. What Sallust either did not see or would not admit is that, bribery apart, the Romans had the soundest of reasons at that moment for avoiding a war in Africa.

* Since this at any rate can hardly be due to Sallust's lack of interest, it is presumably due to lack of information. He cannot have got much from oral tradition, more than sixty years after the events, and his written sources may have been less copious for this particular stage of the war. Some of the later incidents, in which Sulla played an important part, are described in much greater detail, and it has been suggested that Sallust's other documents may have been supplemented here by Sulla's memoirs.

The warlike German tribes known as the Cimbri and Teutoni were on the move: already in 113 B.C., before the Jugurthine war started, the Cimbri had defeated a consular army at Noreia, south of the Danube, whence they turned westward into Switzerland and were soon to appear in Gaul. In these circumstances it may well be argued that, in spite of all Jugurtha's provocation, it was folly for the Romans to undertake the war at all, and that those who wanted to settle with him on any reasonable terms after the first campaign in 111 B.C. were not traitors but sensible men – even if Lucius Bestia had pocketed the king's money.

Sallust writes in a highly individual and somewhat artificial style, mostly in short, terse sentences, packed full of ideas which he seems impatient to express – a style as different from the oratorical rotundity of Cicero as it is from the graceful and flowing copiousness of Livy. He is fond of antithesis (imitating, in this respect at least, the Greek style of Thucydides, whom he greatly admired), but avoids symmetry and smoothness, even to the point of abruptness. His affectation of obsolete words, noted with disapproval by several ancient critics, is a part of his earnest and sometimes even laborious effort to eschew commonplace diction – a characteristic in which he was followed, with brilliant if sometimes disconcerting success, by Tacitus. The set speeches which are supposed to be delivered by Adherbal, Memmius, Marius and others are full of highly polished and effective rhetoric; there is no doubt that – like Thucydides – Sallust composed them himself, embodying the gist of what the speakers actually said if any information about it was available, but for the most part inventing such arguments as it seemed to him probable that they would use.

THE JUGURTHINE WAR

INTRODUCTION

THE GROWTH OF ROMAN POWER

FOUNDED in the eighth century B.C., Rome remained for some centuries an unimportant city-state, subsisting on agriculture. Gradually, however, her influence was extended, first over the neighbouring territory of Latium and the rest of central Italy, and eventually, by the middle of the third century, over the whole peninsula. Alliances were made on varying conditions with many other towns and communities; others were united more closely with Rome herself by the grant of some or all of the rights of Roman citizenship.

A collision with the imperialistic and commercial city of Carthage – resulting from the fact that both Carthage and the Greek cities of southern Italy, now more or less brought under Roman control, had important interests in Sicily – led to the first extension of Roman power beyond the Italian mainland. After the first Carthaginian war (264–241), Sicily and Sardinia-with-Corsica became the first overseas *provinciae* – i.e. governmental areas allotted to Roman magistrates. The Carthaginians then turned their attention to Spain, and in the pursuit of their policy of expansion brought a large part of it under their control. It was from here that Hannibal set out to invade Italy in 218. When the Romans finally prevailed in this exhausting second Carthaginian war, the greater part of Spain was formed into two new provinces, and Rome thus found herself the mistress of the western Mediterranean.

Before long she became involved also in the East, intervening at first to help Greek communities which complained of aggression by King Antiochus of Syria and King Philip of Macedon. But the resulting series of wars ended in the subjugation of the

Greeks themselves: for the Romans at last despaired of the attempt to make them live peaceably with one another, and made their country into the Province of Macedonia. About the same time, a half-century of peace with the Carthaginians was ended by the outbreak of hostilities between them and King Masinissa of Numidia, Rome's ally on their western frontier. This time, the city of Carthage was destroyed and her territory made into the Roman Province of Africa (roughly coextensive with modern Tunisia).*

Thus, in less than a century, Rome had become the greatest imperial power in the world. The possession of six extra-Italian provinces gave her control of the entire Mediterranean and brought her enormous wealth. At the same time it imposed very heavy responsibilities upon her citizens, and created, or aggravated, the difficulties which in the end put an intolerable strain both upon their political, social, and economic institutions and upon their own moral fibre.

THE GOVERNMENT OF REPUBLICAN ROME

The Republic was governed by the *Senatus Populusque Romanus*. The various Assemblies of the People were electoral and legislative bodies. Executive duties were carried out partly by magistrates elected in the Assemblies – the most important being two consuls, a varying number of praetors, and ten tribunes of the plebs, who had special powers, including that of preventing by a veto the transaction of business by any official body or any magistrate except a dictator appointed in an emergency – and partly by the Senate, which was composed of some three hundred ex-magistrates. But for a century or more before 133 B.C. – a year which was to prove a turning-point in Roman history – the Senate had been very much the senior partner in government. Neither the Assemblies nor individual

* This Province was the Roman base of operations in the war with Jugurtha.

magistrates showed much inclination to assert their constitutional powers, at all events in those departments of administration for which the Senate, being the only governmental body which had the necessary capabilities and experience, had assumed responsibility during the long period of war and expansion – that is, in foreign relations, provincial government, finance, and the appointment of military commanders. Even in legislation, in which the powers of the people were in theory unfettered, it was the custom to seek the Senate's approval for most measures before they were submitted to the vote of the Assemblies. Moreover, this far-reaching control was largely concentrated in the hands of an inner circle of senators – men who could boast a consul among their direct ancestors. These were the *nobiles* whom Marius attacked so bitterly in the speech inserted by Sallust in section 85 of his *Jugurthine War*. They belonged to a limited number of families: in the century preceding 133 B.C., twenty-six noble families furnished over three quarters of the consuls elected, and no more than ten families furnished nearly half of them. The aristocracy maintained this influence largely by patronage: so many citizens were dependent on them for the protection of their personal rights and economic interests, that the noblemen could generally count on having a sufficient number of votes in their pockets to secure election in preference to outsiders, more especially to the consulship, which indeed they came to regard as a sort of personal prerogative.

Towards the end of the pre-revolutionary period the nobles themselves began to be divided into two groups – a larger group which came to be called the *optimates* (i.e. supporters of the 'best' men), determined above all to uphold the power of the aristocratic oligarchy, and a smaller group, styled *populares*, or 'demagogues', by their opponents, which included both genuine reformers and ambitious men seeking their own advancement. Since the *optimates* succeeded in retaining firm control of the Senate, the *populares* were driven to seek the support of the people, and for this purpose to use the powers of the tribunes of the plebs, who had the right of initiating legislation in the Assembly. This proved to be political dynamite.

The senators were mainly a landed aristocracy, and were actually forbidden by law to engage in overseas commerce – although this law may often have been evaded. Commerce, banking, contracts for public works, and later the business of tax-farming (for the state maintained only the barest skeleton of permanent officials), were in the hands of the non-senatorial class known as the Equestrian Order, or Equites.* The expansion of the empire greatly increased the wealth and importance of this class, and in the latter half of the second century B.C. they were trying to promote their interests still further by enlarging their political influence and obtaining a share of public administration. In course of time this led to a prolonged struggle between the Equites and the Senate.

In the preface to his *Conspiracy of Catiline*, Sallust has much to say of the contrast between the virtuous Romans of antiquity and the depravity of their successors. No doubt he exaggerates it, like other preachers on similar themes. But it is probable that the political calamities in the last century of the Republic did result to some extent from a deterioration in public and private morality, itself consequent upon the unprecedented opportunities of amassing wealth. War booty, indemnities, overseas trade, money-lending, the proceeds of taxes and the profits of their collection, and sometimes the

* Literally, 'Cavalrymen' – originally men whose means enabled them to serve in the army as cavalrymen at their own expense. But in the second century B.C. the Order included all men registered by the censors as having property sufficient to qualify them for such service, and not belonging to the Senatorial Order – i.e. men of substance who had not held a magistracy entitling them to membership of the Senate. The required amount of property was probably laid down by law.

illegitimate gains of provincial administration, all contributed to the enrichment both of the state and of individual citizens. There is evidence dating from the latter half of the second century B.C. of increasing extravagance and corruption among the ruling class at Rome, especially of direct and indirect bribery of the electorate. The Senate voted more and more money for providing the lavish public games in which the Roman populace delighted, and the magistrates who presided over the festivals added to their magnificence by spending huge sums out of their own pockets on gladiatorial shows and other such spectacles. Worse still, candidates for office resorted more and more as time went on to shameless bribery of electors, in spite of several laws which made this practice punishable. Although the general standard of provincial government seems to have been satisfactory, there were some bad cases of governors who enriched themselves by conniving at illegal exactions on the part of tax-collectors; and to deal with such offences the first permanent criminal court was instituted in 149 B.C. (*quaestio de repetundis*, i.e. a court of inquiry concerning the recovery of property wrongfully extorted).

THE BEGINNING OF THE REVOLUTION

The first serious clash between the Senate and those who sought to challenge its effective control of government arose out of the economic situation in Italy. There had been a time when most of the country was farmed by smallholders. But long periods of compulsory military service had resulted in many holdings' being ruined by neglect, and the growth of large-scale agriculture had rendered it more difficult to make small farms pay – except for corn-growing in the more fertile areas. Meanwhile, the land owned by the state (*ager publicus*), which had been much enlarged during the Hannibalic war by confiscations from disloyal communities, was leased out in big lots – not being required for any other purpose – to men who had enough capital to develop it for stock-raising, viticulture, or olive-growing. So while poor men drifted to Rome to swell the ranks of the urban proletariat, large tracts of land nominally belonging to the state were being profitably farmed, with slave labour, by absentee *entrepreneurs* who appear to have paid little or nothing for the use of it, perhaps because there was no proper machinery for collecting payments of rent. This produced a military as well as a social problem: there was a serious shortage of Roman conscripts with the minimum property qualification which (according to strict rule if not always in practice) was required for service with the legions,* and most of the other Italian communities found it increasingly difficult to produce enough men for the levies demanded of them.

It was in 133 B.C. that Tiberius Sempronius Gracchus, a genuine reformer descended from a noble family, proposed to alleviate the economic distress by reclaiming all *ager publicus* held by private individuals over a certain modest limit and distributing it in small lots to impoverished citizens, who were to pay rent to the treasury. So far as the land reform itself was concerned, he was successful. His *lex agraria* was duly passed, a commission set up to carry it into execution, and a very large number of smallholders installed. But the methods he adopted to effect his reform, and the Senate's reaction to them, did untold harm to the Republic. Instead of trying to obtain a hearing from the Senate, in which there was at any rate a minority of sensible men who might have been willing to accept moderate measures of reform, Tiberius took his bill straight to the Popular Assembly, and when it was vetoed

* This requirement dates from an early period, when Roman citizens served with the colours at their own expense, providing their own equipment. They were registered, according to their means, in various groups, which served as cavalrymen, legionaries, or light-armed troops.

there by another tribune he induced the people to depose him from his office. When Attalus, king of Pergamum in Asia Minor, bequeathed his kingdom and its revenues to the Roman state, Tiberius announced his intention of bringing in a bill to authorize the use of a part of the proceeds to provide capital for the new tenants – a serious encroachment on the Senate's hitherto undisputed control of financial and foreign affairs. Finally he decided to seek election for a second period of office as tribune – a move which, though not illegal, was contrary to custom and was bound to arouse the suspicion that he was aiming at prolonged mob-leadership. These proceedings were admittedly tactless and provocative. But the retaliatory action of a group of senators – taken apparently without protest from their fellow members at the time, and certainly without subsequent punishment – was infinitely worse. Led by Publius Scipio Nasica, head of the College of Pontiffs, they took advantage of some riotous behaviour in the Assembly to massacre Tiberius and three hundred of his supporters. There was no senatorial decree that could possibly be construed into an excuse for this outrage, and it was not even alleged that Tiberius's followers had taken up arms or had any intention of doing so. It was plain political murder, and became a precedent for even worse crimes of the same kind, which in less than half a century led to civil war accompanied by bloodthirsty purges and in the end destroyed the Republic.

Tiberius Gracchus's younger brother Gaius was elected a tribune for the year 123. Some of his wide-ranging proposals, such as the provision of corn at low and fixed prices and the foundation of new citizen colonies in Italy and overseas, were calculated to attract the favour of the city populace. More important measures won the support of the Equites by giving them both further opportunities of making money and an important share of public administration. A system was established whereby the right to collect the taxes of the rich new province of Asia, formed in 129 out of the kingdom of Pergamum, was to be auctioned at Rome by the censors. The successful bidders – and only rich Equites or syndicates formed by them could put up the necessary capital – were to pay a purchase price to the state and seek their profit by retaining the tax-money they collected. Obviously, unscrupulous contractors would be tempted to increase their gains by extorting more than the legal amount of tax from the provincials – a form of oppression that only an honest and alert governor would be able to prevent, since it was not in itself subject to legal prosecution. And even a conscientious governor might well be deterred from interfering with the tax-gatherers by another of Gaius's laws. Hitherto, governors charged with extortion or other acts of maladministration had been tried, in the *quaestio de repetundis*, before juries empanelled from the senators. These might well be disposed to be lenient towards fellow members of their Order, though up to Gaius's time there do not seem to have been any scandalous miscarriages of justice. He now removed control of the court from the Senate by means of a bill enacting that the juries should in future be composed of members of the Equestrian Order. Whether his intention was merely to ingratiate himself with the Equites, or whether he thought it sound policy to enlarge their power at the expense of the Senate's, the change had unfortunate results. For one thing, it enabled members of the Order to retaliate upon a governor who tried to check the activities of predatory tax-farmers, by putting up an accuser to charge him with misgovernment and getting him convicted on slender or even false evidence; and after an initial period during which the Equestrian juries appear to have discharged their duties properly, some notorious instances of such convictions occurred. Another consequence was that the control of this court became a bone of contention that perpetuated strife between senators and

Equites for the next half-century – in fact until the control was divided between them, as it should have been at the start.

After he had held a second tribunate, various circumstances combined to decrease Gaius's popularity, and a group of extremist senators took the opportunity to deal with him as they had dealt with his brother. This time, however, some show of legality was given to their actions by the use of a procedure of which we shall hear much in connexion with the Catilinarian conspiracy. This was a senatorial decree, passed now for the first time, and known as the 'decree concerning the defence of the state' (*senatus consultum de re publica defendenda*), which called upon the consuls and other magistrates 'to see that the state should suffer no injury'. The exact force of this decree was a matter of dispute. Sallust* gives the Optimate view of the matter, alleging that it entitled a magistrate 'to levy troops and conduct war, to apply unlimited force to allies and citizens alike, and to exercise supreme command and jurisdiction both at home and abroad'. According to this theory, it temporarily conferred upon the magistrate legal rights which he did not otherwise possess, by suspending for the time being the laws which secured to all Roman citizens a right to appeal to the People against magisterial decisions affecting their life or person. But this alleged right of the Senate to suspend the law in order to enlarge the magistrates' powers was hotly contested by the Populares, and there can be little doubt that their interpretation was correct in law. According to it, the senatorial decree merely called on the magistrate, in a state of emergency, to use his own discretion in taking measures for the protection of the state. It implied, no doubt, that the Senate was of opinion that it would be justifiable for him, or even incumbent upon him, to disregard for the moment the ordinary legal limitations on the use of his *imperium*; and doubtless there was also an implied assurance that if he were subsequently prosecuted for

* *Catiline*, 29.

acting illegally, he would have the moral support of the Senate in defending himself against such a charge. But the responsibility was his and his alone, and no senatorial decree could relieve him of it. In the case of Gaius Gracchus, the Optimates' action was to some extent justified by the fact that some of his supporters, warned by the fate of Tiberius twelve years before, were rash enough to arm themselves when danger threatened. Lucius Opimius, one of the consuls of 121 B.C., led the attack. Not content with killing Gaius himself, his most prominent supporter Marcus Fulvius Flaccus,* and the others who had taken up arms (these could reasonably be regarded as having forfeited their citizen rights and made themselves enemies of the state), he arrested and executed three thousand of Gaius's followers without any trial worth the name or opportunity of appeal.

Whatever the merits of the questions at issue between the Gracchi and the Optimates, this brutal severity was a blunder. The fact that Opimius (who was put on trial the next year for his part in it) was acquitted by an Assembly of the People is no proof that all his actions were justified by the emergency – though it was afterwards quoted as a precedent by those who maintained that the 'last decree of the Senate' (as it is sometimes called) temporarily conferred on magistrates the right to execute summary justice upon citizens. A Popular politician might have argued that it merely showed how the fickle mob had lost interest in its late champion, and how unworthy a defender it was of its own rights. For the time being the Conservatives thought they had won a famous victory. But they had unsheathed a weapon which their opponents eventually learnt to use against them with deadly effect.

The following decade was comparatively uneventful. The consulship still remained the prerogative of noble families: seven Metelli gained it within the space of fifteen years. These Metelli, who included the Quintus Caecilius Metellus (consul

* See Introduction to the *Catiline*, p. 153.

109) who played an important part in the Jugurthine war, were on the whole intransigent Optimates, though perhaps less prejudiced, and certainly less violent, than the die-hard fire-brands of the period immediately preceding. Another prominent figure in the *Bellum Iugurthinum*, Marcus Aemilius Scaurus (consul 115), appears to have been much more open-minded and progressive. Cicero had a high opinion of him, and Sallust's harsh judgements of his character and motives* are pretty certainly due to misunderstanding, if not to downright prejudice against him. Sallust has much to say of pretence and inconsistency in politics, and seems to have disliked Scaurus, as he evidently disliked Cicero, because he was prepared to change his policies and adapt himself to circumstances. Sallust, apparently, liked a man to be forthright and inflexible of purpose – a last-ditch Conservative like Cato, or an unashamed seeker after popularity and power like Caesar – and was repelled by that willingness to compromise which so often is essential to successful statesmanship because it is the only way of meeting a situation without violent upheaval.

Although the *nobiles* appeared to be still well entrenched in their position of power, they were soon to find themselves involved in a bitter struggle, for their most formidable and ruthless opponent was about to rise up against them. Gaius Marius was a man of the people in every way: born of humble parentage in a country town, he became immensely popular in the ordinary sense of the word, and he supported the 'popular' side in politics. He had served with distinction in a Spanish campaign (133) and held the offices of tribune (119) and praetor (115), after which he went again to Spain as propraetor. Creditable as his career was for an obscure newcomer, there had been nothing particularly remarkable about it. It was the war against the Numidian king Jugurtha, begun in 112, that gave him his real opportunity. In the campaigns of

* See especially section 15^{4-5}.

109 and 108 he did good service as second-in-command to Metellus; but his ambition aimed at more than a subordinate post. For months he kept asking Metellus for leave to go to Rome in order to stand for a consulship, and in spite of snubs and delays he finally got his way. It was an opportune moment for him. For four years Jugurtha had defied the might of Rome. Many leading senators were believed to have accepted his bribes, and even some of the aristocratic generals who had conducted the first campaigns against him were suspected of treason. In any case, they had been incompetent; and although Metellus himself was an honest and capable commander, the war still dragged on. Thus Marius, in attacking the selfishness and ineffectiveness of the nobility, had an easy target, and he was successful in his candidature for one of the consulships of 107. Thereupon the People transferred the African command to him in defiance of a senatorial decree which had reappointed Metellus. Robbed in this way of one of their most cherished and hitherto unchallenged privileges – the selection of military commanders – the senatorial nobility had no alternative but to acquiesce for the time being. But they had not finally accepted defeat; and when eventually they found a champion prepared to fight for them Rome was plunged into civil war.

THE ROMAN ARMY

Up to the time of Marius, the Roman legions were a conscript militia.* Marius turned them into regiments of semi-professional soldiers by recruiting any able-bodied citizens willing to serve.† The most important tactical units had hitherto been the thirty maniples into which each legion was divided – companies of varying strength (generally about 120 men), each of which had its own *signum* or standard and consisted of

* See above, pp. 19–20.

† *Jugurthine War*, section 86.

two centuries, or sections. When circumstances required a larger unit, cohorts – battalions comprising three maniples – had sometimes been used; and in the first century B.C. the cohort, now with a nominal strength of 600 men, became the standard tactical unit, though it was still divided into maniples and centuries. Marius is supposed to have introduced this change, but it is not certain that it was fully established in his lifetime. There are only two passages in the *Jugurthine War* where cohorts of legionaries are certainly referred to: one (51[3]) in Metellus's first campaign, and one (100[4]) in Marius's second campaign.

In the Republican period legions had no commanders other than the consul or proconsul who was commander-in-chief for the time being, or his deputy. Each legion had six military tribunes,* who were often young aspirants to a public career. They would usually have had some experience of warfare, which they often obtained by serving as orderlies in attendance on a commander or other officer.† The tribunes' duties, which were both administrative and active, were assigned to them by the commander-in-chief or his lieutenants (*legati*). The latter were men of senatorial rank. Metellus's lieutenants in his African campaigns were Marius and Publius Rutilius Rufus; when Marius became commander, his lieutenant was Aulus Manlius. The commander was assisted also by a quaestor, who, in addition to administrative duties such as those of a paymaster, usually took command in his chief's absence. Sulla was Marius's quaestor in Africa. The non-commissioned officers of the legions – though they must often have discharged duties which in a modern army are assigned to company officers – were called centurions; these were ex-rankers, promoted for

* For the four legions which were ordinarily raised each year, military tribunes were elected by the People (section 63[4]). If additional legions were recruited, the consul in command appointed tribunes for them.

† Metellus had his son in attendance upon him in Numidia (section 64[4]).

bravery and powers of leadership to the command of centuries. There were sixty in a legion, including a chief centurion,* who held a very responsible position and was regularly summoned with the lieutenants and military tribunes to the commander's council of war.

The legions were supported by bodies of non-citizen troops supplied by Italian communities, properly called *socii*, or 'allies', and also by contingents of foreigners. Sallust's terminology is often inexact in his references to various classes of troops. He uses the word *auxilia* for both Italian *socii* and foreigners; *cohortes* for both legionary cohorts and cohorts of Italian infantry; *turmae*, or 'squadrons', for both Italian and foreign cavalry. Apart from the cavalry, the foreigners mentioned in the *Jugurthine War* were companies of slingers.

We do not know in much detail how the legionaries were armed at this particular time. For close fighting they had pointed two-edged swords, but for opening an engagement most, if not all, of them carried heavy throwing-spears, sometimes nearly seven feet long, and so made that the iron head bent when it pierced an enemy's shield.† In the second century the legionary's shield was oval; in or soon after Marius's time, a curved rectangular shield was substituted.

THE KINGDOM OF NUMIDIA

Numidia stretched for nearly seven hundred miles along the North African coast, being bounded on the west by the River Muluccha (Moulouya), which separated it from Morocco, and on the east by the Carthaginian territory which in 146 B.C. became the Roman Province of Africa. Thus it coincided approximately with what is now Algeria and the western part of Tunisia. Apart from the fertile coastal plains, it is a rugged mountainous country, and although the Romans did not

* Section 38[6].

† This improvement in the specification of the *pilum* is attributed to Marius.

penetrate into the huge Atlas plateau which stretches southwards to the desert, their campaigns being mostly confined to Old Numidia (roughly the modern province of Constantine together with Western Tunisia), even here they had to march in the heat of summer over a terrain rising to several thousand feet, where with their heavy equipment they were at a serious disadvantage against the lightly-equipped, mobile armies of the natives.

The Numidians, as well as the Moors who lived west of them, belonged mostly to the race from which the Berbers are descended. Their name meant Nomads, and for a long time the population consisted mainly of small clans of nomadic herdsmen. The most famous man in their history was King Masinissa, who ruled throughout the first half of the second century B.C. He greatly enlarged the frontiers of his kingdom – extending it south and east so as to surround Carthage on the land side, and occupying the ports of Tripolitania – and converted his people into a settled agricultural community, with many thriving towns and a civilization derived largely from their Carthaginian neighbours. As a young man he became an ally of Rome, and their common hostility towards Carthage preserved this friendship intact for half a century. His death in 148 B.C., at the age of ninety, was soon followed by the final destruction of Carthage, which removed the strong motive for Numidian loyalty to Rome. The next ruler was his son Micipsa, and it was Micipsa's death (118 B.C.) that started the series of events, described in detail by Sallust, which established Jugurtha on the throne.

THE COURSE OF THE WAR

Sallust's chronology is often so vague that we cannot tell exactly when events occurred, and sometimes it is not even clear in what order they occurred. Some of the dates given below, therefore, are by no means certain.

There were three phases of the war, each occupying approximately two years:

I. *The First Campaigns: Roman Failures*

112 B.C. Fall of Cirta and murder of Adherbal (section 26)
111 Bestia's campaign (28); abortive settlement with Jugurtha (29; 32)
[111–110 Jugurtha's visit to Rome (33–5)]
110 Campaign of Spurius Albinus (36); campaign and capitulation of Aulus Albinus (37–8)
[110 or 109 Lex Mamilia (40)]

II. *Metellus's Campaigns: Indecisive Roman Successes*

109 B.C. Occupation of Vaga (section 47); battle at the River Muthul (48–53); unsuccessful siege of Zama (56–61); rising at Vaga (66–9)
108 Capture of Thala (75–6); occupation of Cirta (81)

III. *Marius's Campaigns: Final Roman Victory*

107 B.C. Capture of Capsa (sections 89–91)
107–106 Reduction of many Numidian strongholds (92)
106 Capture of fortress on the River Muluccha (92–4); arrival of Sulla in Africa with cavalry (95); two battles with Jugurtha and Bocchus (97–101)
106–105 Winter quarters in coastal towns (100; 103); capture of a royal castle (103); negotiations with Bocchus (102–11)
105 Bocchus's betrayal of Jugurtha to Sulla (112–13)

Some ancient and modern writers have thought that Metellus had victory within his grasp when he was superseded at the end of 108 B.C., and that all Marius had to do was to carry on with his predecessor's plan of campaign. Others maintain that Marius was the real author of the Roman victory. The question is not easy for a modern reader to decide from Sallust's incomplete and sometimes confused account of the military operations; but it is certain that Marius's contemporaries gave him the chief credit: for on the strength of the reputation he won in this war he was regarded as the obvious choice for the much more important command against the German invaders in the north, and was elected to an unprecedented – and indeed unconstitutional – series of five consulships (104–100 B.C.).

Metellus was intelligent enough to see what the situation required. He realized quite soon that it was of little use to win battles, as long as Jugurtha could replace the troops he lost. So he marched about the country doing all the damage he could, to intimidate the population, and destroyed a number of lightly defended places. But this process was likely to prove tedious, and even if he succeeded in driving the king out of Old Numidia into the western part of his kingdom, Jugurtha might still be able to carry on hostilities as long as he was at large; the only short way, and the only certain way, was to kill or capture him. So Metellus found means to corrupt Jugurtha's confidant Bomilcar, who undertook to find some way of doing it. The plan very nearly succeeded. Jugurtha was persuaded to throw himself on Metellus's mercy, and actually surrendered his elephants and a quantity of money, horses, and arms; but at the last moment, Sallust says, 'his guilty conscience made him fear the punishment that he deserved', and he changed his mind. Persuasion having failed, Bomilcar and some other Numidian courtiers tried to earn the rewards Metellus had offered them by plotting to seize the king's person and either to kill him or surrender him to the Romans. When this also miscarried, Metellus tried to do the job himself by making a sudden descent on the desert town of Thala, where Jugurtha had taken refuge; but the king escaped in time with his family and a large part of his treasure, and thereafter kept constantly on the move. Still determined to resist, he enlisted a fresh army of Gaetulian mercenaries from the Sahara; and when the loss of most of his treasure made it impossible for him to pay these any longer, he induced his son-in-law Bocchus, king of the Moors, to agree to join in the fight against the Romans. It was now near the end of the year 108, and Metellus had made little progress towards achieving his object. His well-laid plans had failed because the luck was against him and because Jugurtha was too clever. Now, without any warning (for the Senate had already assigned him the Numidian command for a further year), he found himself superseded by his lieutenant Marius.

The new consul had a larger force at his disposal than his predecessor, and was a more energetic and adventurous commander. He was faced with a situation quite as difficult as that which had faced Metellus. Although the greater part of Jugurtha's Numidian army had broken up, in consequence of wholesale desertions after its defeat and the loss of nearly all his reliable officers, the king had now trained his Gaetulian recruits; and if Bocchus could be persuaded to commit himself to war, his Moors would be a powerful reinforcement, which would make Marius's task much more formidable. It was essential, therefore, either to deter Bocchus from entering the war, or if this proved impossible, to induce him to desert his ally; and the only way of doing this would be to convince him that Jugurtha could not win, even with his help, and that he himself would stand to gain by deserting his ally. By attacking as many Numidian strongholds as possible, Marius hoped either to tempt Jugurtha to risk pitched battles or to strip him of the means of defending the most important part of his kingdom. To facilitate this purpose, he made a swift march across the desert to the large town of Capsa, on the southern edge of Old Numidia, took it by surprise, burnt it, and killed or enslaved its inhabitants. This act of terrorism intimidated the Numidians into evacuating many towns, and others, which resisted, were captured by assault. Sallust gives no details, but there was probably a large number of these places, and their reduction apparently occupied the last months of 107 and a considerable part of 106. Marius then undertook a daring six-hundred mile march westwards to the River Muluccha, on the Moroccan frontier, to attack a mountain fortress which contained the king's largest treasury, and captured it, according to Sallust, more by good luck than anything else.

Jugurtha was now pretty well excluded from Old Numidia, and no doubt the continuance of the war and the loss of a large part of his treasure made it difficult for him to keep his troops in service. He therefore decided to risk everything on battle, and at last, by the offer of a third part of his kingdom, he induced Bocchus (who was still sitting on the fence) to join him. The two kings engaged the whole Roman army twice within a few days, and in the second battle came within an ace of defeating it. But after a long and bloody fight Marius was, as Sallust puts it, 'victor beyond question'. It only remained for Marius's quaestor Sulla, by playing skilfully on the ambitions and fears of Bocchus, to argue him into trapping Jugurtha and delivering him up in chains. Jugurtha was carried to Rome, and after appearing in Marius's triumph died in prison. Bocchus received western Numidia as the price of his treachery, while the eastern half of the kingdom was given to Jugurtha's half-brother Gauda.

CHAPTER I

PREFACE

MEN have no right to complain that they are naturally feeble and short-lived, or that it is chance and not merit that decides their destiny. On the contrary, reflection will show that nothing exceeds or surpasses the powers with which nature has endowed mankind, and that it is rather energy they lack than strength or length of days. What guides and controls human life is man's soul. If it pursues glory by the path of virtue, it has all the resources and abilities it needs for winning fame, and is independent of fortune, which can neither give any man uprightness, energy, and other good qualities, nor deprive any man of them. But if the soul is enslaved by base desires and sinks into the corruption of sloth and carnal pleasures, it enjoys a ruinous indulgence for a brief season; then, when idleness has wasted strength, youth, and intelligence, the blame is put on the weakness of our nature, and each man excuses himself for his own shortcomings by imputing his failure to adverse circumstances. If men pursued good things with the same ardour with which they seek what is unedifying and unprofitable – often, indeed, actually dangerous and pernicious – they would control events instead of being controlled by them, and would rise to such heights of greatness and glory that their mortality would put on immortality.

As man consists of body and soul, all our possessions and pursuits partake of the nature of one or the other. Thus personal beauty and great wealth, bodily strength, and all similar things, soon pass away; the noble achievements of the intellect are immortal like the soul itself. Physical advantages, and the material gifts of fortune, begin and end; all that comes into existence, perishes; all that grows, must one day decay. But the soul, incorruptible and eternal, is the ruler of mankind; it guides and controls everything, subject itself to no control. Wherefore we can but marvel the more at the unnatural conduct of those who abandon themselves to bodily pleasures and pass their time in riotous living and idleness, neglecting their intelligence – the best and noblest element in man's nature – and letting it become dull through lack of effort; and that, too, when the mind is capable of so many different accomplishments that can win the highest distinction.

Of these various paths to fame, it seems to me that the holding of civil and military posts, and indeed all political activities, are in these days the least desirable. For the deserving do not obtain the honours of office; and the ill-deservers who do obtain them gain nothing thereby either in security or in true honour. The use of force to rule one's country or subjects – even if a man is in a position of power, and employs that power to right wrongs – is a perilous course: for it invites counter-measures, and any attempt at revolution is a certain forerunner of massacre, banishment, and other acts of warlike violence. On the other hand, to struggle in vain against odds, and after exhausting efforts to gain nothing but hatred, is the height of folly – a folly that no one is likely to be guilty of, unless he is possessed by a dishonourable and fatal desire to sacrifice his own honour and freedom in order to increase the power of a set of oligarchs.

Among intellectual pursuits, one of the most useful is the recording of past events. As many have spoken of its value, I think it best to remain silent on the subject – especially as someone might think that vanity was making me sing the praises of my own favourite occupation. I do not doubt that some people, because I have determined to keep aloof from politics, will describe the arduous and profitable task I am undertaking as a lazy man's amusement. It will certainly seem so to those whose idea of hard work is to court the rabble and curry favour by lavish entertaining. But I would ask them to consider what eminent men failed to obtain election to magistracies in the period when I held mine; and, on the other hand, what kinds of men have since gained admission to the Senate. If they will do so, they will surely conclude that I had good reason for altering my opinion about politics, that it was not mere laziness, and that more profit is likely to accrue to the state from my leisured retirement than from the busy activity of others.

I have often heard that Quintus Maximus,* Publius Scipio,* and other illustrious citizens of our state, used to say that the sight of their ancestors' portrait-masks† fired their hearts with an ardent desire to merit honour. Obviously they did not mean that the actual mould of wax had such power over them, but that the memory of what others have accomplished kindles in the breasts of noble men a flame that is not quenched until their own prowess has won similar glory and renown. In these degenerate days, however, one cannot find a man who does not seek to rival his ancestors in wealth and extravagance, instead of in uprightness and industry. Even newcomers to politics, who formerly relied on merit to outstrip the nobility, now use underhand intrigue and open violence, instead of honourable means, in the struggle for military and civil power, as though a praetorship, a consulship, or any similar position, were something glorious and magnificent in itself – whereas, in reality, the respect in which such offices are held depends on the worth of those who uphold their dignity. However, I have allowed myself to be carried too far in expressing the loathing and distaste which I feel for our standard of public morality. I will now return to the task that I have undertaken.

I propose to write an account of the war which the Romans

* See note on section 5[4].

† Wax death-masks of ancestors who had held high office. They were kept by Romans in their houses, and were worn by actors at the funerals of distinguished members of the family.

fought with Jugurtha king of Numidia: first, because it was a hard-fought and bloody contest in which victories alternated with defeats; secondly, because it was at this time that the first challenge was offered to the arrogance of the Roman nobles – the beginning of a struggle that played havoc with all our institutions, human and divine, and reached such a pitch of fury that civil strife was ended only by a war which left Italy a desert. But before explaining how Rome came to be involved in this bitter fight with Jugurtha, I will go back to certain earlier events in order to set my narrative in a clearer light and make it more readily understood.

CHAPTER II

EARLY LIFE OF JUGURTHA

DURING the second Punic war, in which the Carthaginian commander Hannibal had dealt Italy the severest blows it had ever suffered since Rome became a great nation,* the Numidian king Masinissa was admitted to Roman friendship by Publius Scipio, whose high qualities later gained him the title 'Africanus'. Masinissa achieved many brilliant military successes, for which – after the defeat of Carthage and the capture of Syphax, the possessor of a vast and powerful empire in Africa – he was rewarded by the Romans with a gift of all the cities and territories that he had taken in the war. Consequently, Masinissa remained a loyal and true friend to Rome until his rule ended with his death.† Eventually his son Micipsa became the sole ruler, because his brothers Mastanabal and Gulussa died of disease. He had two children of his own, Adherbal and Hiempsal; and Jugurtha, his brother Mastanabal's illegitimate son, whom Masinissa's will had excluded from the succession on account of his birth, was kept in the palace and treated in the same way as Micipsa's own sons.

As soon as Jugurtha grew up, endowed as he was with great strength and handsome looks, but above all with a powerful intellect, he did not let himself be spoiled by luxury or idleness,

* In the great Carthaginian war of 218–202 B.C., Hannibal, who had invaded Italy by marching from Spain across the Alps, won several spectacular victories over the Roman armies, but was at length foiled by the evasive strategy of Quintus Fabius Maximus, nicknamed the Delayer. Eventually Publius Cornelius Scipio's invasion of Carthage's home territory forced him to return to Africa, where he was defeated in the decisive battle of Zama.

† On Masinissa see Introduction, p. 29. Syphax, ruler of the western part of Numidia, changed sides more than once but eventually took the Carthaginian side against Masinissa and the Romans, who defeated and captured him (203 B.C.).

but took part in the national pursuits of riding and javelin-throwing and competed with other young men in running; and though he outshone them all he was universally beloved. He also devoted much time to hunting, and was always to the fore at the killing of lions and other wild beasts. His energy was equalled by his modesty: he never boasted of his exploits. Micipsa was at first pleased with the way his nephew distinguished himself, thinking that it would add lustre to his reign; but when he realized that Jugurtha, in the prime of his young manhood, was continually increasing his prestige, while he himself was old and his children still small, he became very anxious and pondered much upon the situation. There were several disquieting features. Men, he reflected, are naturally greedy for power and impatient to satisfy their desires; his own age and that of his children might make it seem easy to seize a prize worth having – and such opportunities tempt even the unambitious to swerve from the path of rectitude; the Numidians, too, were fond of Jugurtha, and to have such a man assassinated might well provoke a rebellion or even a civil war.

Unable to see any other way out of these difficulties – since it was clear that neither force nor stratagem could be used to make away with such a popular hero – Micipsa decided to take advantage of Jugurtha's energetic nature and thirst for military glory by exposing him to the perils of war: it might be, he thought, that fortune would come to his aid. The Roman war against Numantia* gave him his chance. He was sending a force of cavalry and infantry to help the Romans, and in the confident hope that Jugurtha would fall a victim either to his own bravado or to the ruthlessness of the enemy, he sent him to Spain in command of the Numidian contingent. But the result was very different from what he expected. Jugurtha, with

* A town on the River Douro in northern Spain. After resisting Roman attacks for over sixty years, it was taken by siege, in 133 B.C., by Publius Cornelius Scipio Aemilianus, grandson by adoption of Hannibal's conqueror.

his active and penetrating mind, grasped the character of Scipio, the Roman commander, and the fighting-methods of the Numantines. Then, by dint of hard work and careful attention to duty, by unquestioning obedience and the readiness with which he exposed himself to risk, he soon won such renown as to become the idol of the Roman soldiers and the terror of the enemy. He was in fact both a tough fighter and a wise counsellor – qualities extremely hard to combine: for generally speaking, a man who looks ahead is timid, while a bold man tends to be rash. Scipio therefore employed him in nearly every difficult task, treated him as a friend, and regarded him each day more highly, as a man who never erred in his judgement and never failed in anything he undertook. Jugurtha had also a generous nature and a shrewd intellect – qualities which won for him the close friendship of quite a number of the Romans.

At this time there were many serving in the Roman army – both men of undistinguished birth and members of the aristocracy – who cared more for wealth than for right and honour, and who, by their party intrigues at home and the influence they had secured in the provinces, had obtained notoriety without deserving respect. These men kindled Jugurtha's ambitious spirit by assuring him that if Micipsa died he would become the sole ruler of Numidia: his own great merits, they said, entitled him to the position, and at Rome money could buy anything.

When Numantia had been destroyed, Publius Scipio resolved to disband his auxiliary troops and return home. After presenting gifts to Jugurtha and commending him in the highest terms before the assembled soldiers, Scipio took him into his headquarters and in a private interview advised him to cultivate the friendship of the Roman commonwealth rather than that of individual Romans, and not to make a habit of offering bribes. It was dangerous, he said, to buy from a few what belonged to many. If Jugurtha would persevere in the good conduct for which he was known, he had only to wait for fame and a royal throne to fall into his lap; but if he was in too great a hurry for advancement, his own money would bring about his fall. After making these remarks Scipio dismissed him with a letter to the following effect, to be delivered to Micipsa:

> Your nephew Jugurtha has distinguished himself in the Numantine war above everyone else, which I am sure will give you pleasure. I hold him in affection for his services, and I will do all I can to make him equally esteemed by the Roman Senate and People. As your friend, I congratulate you personally; you have in him a man worthy of yourself and of his grandfather Masinissa.

Thus Micipsa found the reports which had reached him about Jugurtha confirmed by the Roman commander's letter, and he was much impressed by this proof of his nephew's ability and by the credit he had earned. He therefore changed his mind, and, in an attempt to win him over by favours, lost no time in adopting him and naming him in his will as joint heir with his own sons.*

* This seems to be contradicted by Sallust's own statement in section 11[6] that Jugurtha was adopted as an heir only during the last three years of Micipsa's life.

CHAPTER III

JUGURTHA'S RISE TO POWER (118–116 B.C.)

SOME years later, when he was enfeebled by illness and old age and realized that his end was near, Micipsa expressed a wish to see Jugurtha, and in the presence of a number of friends and relatives, including his sons Adherbal and Hiempsal, he addressed the young man – so it is said – in some such terms as these:

'You were a little child, Jugurtha, fatherless and without resources or prospects, when I received you into the royal household, in the belief that the obligations under which I placed you would make you love me as much as any sons I might have of my own. In this I was not mistaken. For – to say nothing of the fine achievements already standing to your credit – on your return from Numantia you covered me and my kingdom with glory. Your prowess in battle has greatly strengthened the bond of friendship between us and the Romans, and in Spain you revived the reputation of our family. Furthermore, you have done a most difficult thing: by your brilliant success you have silenced the voice of envy. And now, since nature is bringing my life to a close, I earnestly implore you by this hand of yours that I hold, and by the loyalty you owe to our kingdom, to love these boys who are your kinsmen by birth and your brothers by my act of adoption: do not seek to form unions with strangers in preference to cherishing your blood relations. Neither armies nor hoards of treasure can protect a throne, but only friends – and friends one cannot make by force of arms or buy with money: they must be won by devoted service and loyalty. And who can be a closer friend than one brother to another? What stranger will you find loyal, if you are the enemy of your own kindred? The kingdom I bequeath to you and your brothers will be secure if you act honourably, but if you prove false it cannot stand. For concord turns weakness into strength, whereas by discord the greatest resources are dissipated. However, it is not these boys, but you, Jugurtha – since you are older and wiser than they – whose duty it is to see to it that things do not go wrong. Whenever conflict arises, the more powerful disputant, even if he be the victim of injustice, is regarded as the aggressor just because he *is* more powerful. As for you, Adherbal and Hiempsal, respect and honour this good man: emulate his virtues, and try hard to give the world no cause to say that my adopted son is a better man than the sons I have fathered.'

Jugurtha realized the hollowness of the king's words, and he had very different designs in his own mind. Nevertheless, he made a gracious reply, suitable to the occasion. Micipsa died a few days later.* After celebrating his obsequies with royal magnificence, the princes met together for a general discussion of the situation. Hiempsal, the youngest of the three, who was of an arrogant nature and had long despised Jugurtha for his low descent on his mother's side, seated himself on Adherbal's right to prevent Jugurtha from taking the middle seat, which Numidians regard as the place of honour. His brother repeatedly asked him to make way for his senior, and eventually, with a very bad grace, he consented to move to the other side. There was a long debate on the government of the kingdom, during which Jugurtha, among other proposals, suggested the cancellation of all rulings and decrees made within the last five years, on the ground that Micipsa's mental powers had been impaired by senility. Hiempsal said he quite agreed with this suggestion – as it was less than three years since Jugurtha himself, by his uncle's act of adoption, had become entitled to a share of the kingdom. This repartee sank deeper into Jugurtha's mind than anyone realized. It made him both angry and afraid, and

* 118 B.C.

from that moment he began to scheme and plot, thinking of nothing else but of finding some underhand means of getting the better of Hiempsal. But an opportunity was slow in coming; and as his proud spirit was still full of rancour, he resolved to execute his design by any means that offered.

At the meeting to which I have referred, the princes had failed to reach agreement and had therefore decided to divide the royal treasures and partition the kingdom among them. Times were fixed for both distributions, that for the sharing out of the money being the earlier. Before the date appointed, each of them made his way to a different spot in the neighbourhood of the treasury. It happened that Hiempsal, who had gone to the town of Thirmida, was occupying a house belonging to Jugurtha's most confidential attendant, who had always enjoyed his master's favour and esteem. Since chance enabled him to use this man as a tool, Jugurtha induced him by means of lavish promises to go to the house on the pretext of inspecting his property, and to make duplicate keys for the doors – since the original keys were always handed over to Hiempsal. As for the rest, Jugurtha undertook to come himself at the proper time with a strong force. The Numidian carried out his instructions promptly, and duly admitted Jugurtha's soldiers by night. Rushing into the house, they scattered in search of the prince. Some of his servants were killed in their sleep, others in attempts at resistance. Possible hiding-places were ransacked, closed doors broken down, and the whole place filled with noise and confusion. Eventually Hiempsal was found hiding in a maidservant's quarters, where he had taken refuge in his first alarm, not knowing his way about the house. In accordance with their orders the Numidians carried his head to Jugurtha.

The news of this hideous crime spread quickly all over North Africa. Adherbal and all Micipsa's former subjects were terrified. The Numidians now divided into two parties: the majority sided with Adherbal, but the best soldiers favoured his rival. Jugurtha armed as many men as he could, obtained control of various towns by force or persuasion, and prepared to make himself ruler of all Numidia. Adherbal, although he had already sent envoys to Rome to inform the Senate of his brother's assassination and his own precarious plight, was emboldened by confidence in his numerical strength to take the field at once. But he was defeated in the first battle and fled, first to the Roman Province,* thence to Rome.

* The Province of Africa, which was formed from the territory possessed by Carthage at the time of its overthrow in 146 B.C., consisted of a part of modern Tunisia.

CHAPTER IV

JUGURTHA'S DEFIANCE OF ROME (116–112 B.C.)

JUGURTHA had carried out his design, and found himself master of the whole country. But when he had leisure to reflect on what he had done, he began to be afraid of the reaction of the Roman people. His only hope of escaping the consequences of their anger was to take advantage of the avarice of the Roman nobles by using his riches to corrupt them. Accordingly, before many days had passed, he sent ambassadors to Rome with a quantity of gold and silver, directing them to start by loading his old friends with presents, and then to acquire new friends and to lose no time in obtaining any help that money could buy. When they reached Rome, and in compliance with his wishes sent valuable gifts to the king's former hosts and to others whose influence in the Senate was powerful at that time, such a change of sentiment took place among the noblemen that their bitter resentment against Jugurtha was converted into favour and good will. In return for the presents they had received or hoped to receive, they went round canvassing individual senators to prevent any severe measures' being taken against him. When his ambassadors felt confident of success they made application to the Senate, and a day was appointed for hearing both parties to the dispute. This is what Adherbal is reported to have said:

'Members of the Senate, my father Micipsa advised me on his deathbed to consider that it was merely a stewardship of the Numidian kingdom that belonged to me, and that the real ownership and sovereignty of it were yours. He also bade me strive to serve the Roman people to the best of my ability in peace and war, and to regard you as my kinsmen and relatives.

If I did this, he said, your friendship would protect my kingdom as effectually as an army and a treasury. I was trying to carry out my father's injunctions, when Jugurtha, wickedest of all men on the face of the earth, showed his contempt for your imperial power by driving me, a grandson of Masinissa and hereditary ally and friend of the Roman people, from my throne and all my possessions.

'Since such grievous misery was destined to be my lot, gentlemen, I only wish that in asking your help I could point to services which I myself had rendered to you, rather than to those rendered by my ancestors. It would be best of all if the Roman people owed me favours that I stood in no need of; at least, if I must ask favours, I wish I could claim them as my due. But since honesty is little protection in itself, and since I cannot help Jugurtha's being what he is, I am seeking asylum with you, gentlemen; and it is a great grief to me that I am forced to be a burden to you before I can do you any service.

'The other kings who have been admitted to your friendship had either been vanquished by you or sought your alliance at a time when their own position was insecure. Our family established friendly relations with Rome during the Carthaginian war, when your fortunes were at a low ebb and you had little to offer but the steadfastness of a faithful ally. I am a member of that family, gentlemen, and a grandson of Masinissa. Do not let me beg your aid in vain. Had I no other claim to a favourable answer than my pitiable lot – I who was but yesterday a king of distinguished ancestry, fame, and fortune, and now am dishonoured by affliction, destitute, and dependent upon foreign assistance – it would still befit the dignity of Rome to defend me from this wrong: for no prince should be permitted to enlarge his dominions by a criminal act. But there is another reason. The kingdom from which I have been expelled is the kingdom that was given to my ancestors by the Roman government, the kingdom from which my father and my grandfather helped you to drive out Syphax and the Carthaginians. It is your gifts, gentlemen, that have been wrested from me. It is you who are insulted in the wrong done to me. Alas, my father Micipsa, is this what has resulted from your generous act in placing Jugurtha on an equality with your children and making him a joint heir of your kingdom – that he, of all men, should be the annihilator of your race? Never, it seems, is our family to be at peace. Evermore must bloodshed, war, and exile be our lot. While the power of Carthage was unbroken, we could not complain of the cruel treatment we endured. The enemy beset us all round; you, our only friends, were far away; and we had no hope but in our arms. When Africa was freed from the Carthaginian scourge, we enjoyed the blessings of peace, with no enemies except those whom you bade us treat as such. Then lo and behold! Jugurtha had arisen, and in his reckless arrogance committed crimes beyond endurance. He started by murdering my brother, his own cousin, and seizing his kingdom as so much plunder. I was too cautious to fall into an assassin's trap, and thought that under the protection of your empire I was safe from aggression. Yet, as you see, he has found means to make me an exile from my home and country. Destitute and overwhelmed with misfortunes, I am safer anywhere than in my own kingdom.

'I always believed my father's assurance that those who diligently cultivated your friendship were recompensed for the arduous tasks they had to perform by the enjoyment of unequalled security. Our family has done what it could for you by aiding you in all your wars. Now that there is peace, we want to live in security, and our chance of doing so, gentlemen, depends on you. My father had two sons, and adopted Jugurtha as a third, hoping that the kindnesses he showed him would unite him to us. Thus I had two brothers. Now, one of them has been killed, and I myself was hard put to it to escape the clutches of his unnatural murderer. What am I to do? What refuge am I to choose in my hapless condition? None of those who might have saved our house remains alive. My father reached the natural term of his life. My brother was foully slain by his cousin, the very last man who should have raised a hand against him. All my relatives by marriage, all my friends and other connexions, have been destroyed in one way or another. They were taken by Jugurtha, and some have been crucified, others thrown to wild beasts; a few whose lives were spared are shut up in gloomy dungeons, and with sorrow and lamentation drag out an existence worse than death itself. Even if I still possessed all the resources that I have lost and all the natural supporters who have turned against me, even so, in the event of any unlooked-for misfortune, I should entreat you, gentlemen, to help me: for the masters of such a mighty empire ought to defend justice and punish wrongdoing. As things are, exiled from my hearth and home, forsaken, stripped of everything that becomes my station, where else can I go, to whom else can I appeal? All peoples and princes are enemies of my family, because we are your friends. Is there any land where I should not find many a reminder that my forefathers once made war on its inhabitants? No one who has ever been at war with Rome will have compassion on us Numidians. Moreover, gentlemen, Masinissa instructed us to seek the friendship of no one but the Roman people, and not to contract any new alliances or treaties: all the protection we could need, he said, would be given us by our friendship with you; and if Fortune ever deserted the Roman empire, we must be prepared to fall with it. In the meantime, thanks to your own merits and the favour of the gods, you are great and prosperous; and the world-wide influence and dominion you have won make it easy for you to redress the wrongs done to your allies.

'My only fear is lest some of you may be led astray by

personal friendship with Jugurtha, not knowing what his friendship is worth. I hear that his supporters are making great efforts, going round and importuning each one of you to decide nothing in Jugurtha's absence and without hearing his case. I am making up a tale, they say, and pretending to be an exile when there was really nothing to prevent my remaining in my kingdom. If this is pretence, I only hope I may live to see a similar pretence being made by the man whose impious deed has plunged me into these misfortunes. May the day come when either you Romans or the immortal gods begin to take some thought for the fortunes of men! Then indeed would that villain, who now prides himself on the success of his crimes, be racked with suffering and pay a heavy penalty for his unfilial conduct towards our father, for the murder of my brother, and for all my distresses.

'O brother dear to my heart, although you were slain before your time by him who of all men should have been the last to do such a deed, I think now that your fate is a happy, not a grievous one. Death did not rob you of a throne: rather did it spare you the endurance of flight, exile, poverty, and all the woes that weigh me down. I am the luckless one. Cast down from an ancestral throne into the depths of calamity, I am an object-lesson of the mutability of human fortunes. I know not what to do. Shall I try to avenge your wrongs when I myself stand in such sore need of succour? Or try to save my kingdom, when my royal power to put to death or to spare depends on foreign aid? Would that to die, and have done with it, were an honourable way of escape from such a position as mine! But people would think I merited contempt, if I were so worn out by my troubles that I could no longer fight against injustice. So I cannot either live with pleasure or die without disgrace.

'Members of the Senate, I conjure you, as you respect yourselves, your children, your parents, and the majesty of the

Roman people – aid me in my affliction, set your faces against injustice, and do not let the kingdom of Numidia, which is your property, be destroyed by the criminal action of a member of its royal family in shedding his kinsman's blood.'

On the conclusion of the king's speech the envoys of Jugurtha, who relied more on bribery than the soundness of their case, made a brief reply. They maintained that Hiempsal had been killed by the Numidians because of his cruelty. As for Adherbal, he had been guilty of aggression; and now that he was beaten, he was complaining because his injurious attempt had failed. 'Jugurtha asks you,' they said, 'not to let anyone persuade you that he is not still the same loyal ally he showed himself to be at Numantia, and not to attach more weight to an enemy's assertions than to his own actions.' Both parties then left the senate house, and the Senate proceeded forthwith to debate the matter. Jugurtha's supporters, as well as a large number of other senators whom their influence had perverted, poured scorn on what Adherbal had said, and highly praised the merits of Jugurtha, using all their interest and eloquence and working as hard to secure impunity for another man's infamous crime as if their own honour had been at stake. In opposition to them, a few who valued right and justice above money recommended that help should be sent to Adherbal, and the murder of Hiempsal punished with the utmost vigour. Conspicuous among these last was Aemilius Scaurus, an enterprising nobleman who, although he was a political intriguer with an appetite for power, advancement, and riches, had enough cunning to hide his faults.* Jugurtha's shameless bribery was notorious, and such an open and scandalous abuse could hardly fail to arouse popular resentment. So for once Scaurus curbed his habitual rapacity.

However, the day was carried by that party in the Senate which was prepared to sacrifice honesty to money or favour.

* See Introduction, p. 25.

It was decreed that ten commissioners should divide between Jugurtha and Adherbal the kingdom formerly ruled by Micipsa. At their head was Lucius Opimius, an eminent man who was then very influential in the Senate because during his consulship, after the assassination of Gaius Gracchus and Marcus Fulvius Flaccus, he had ruthlessly exploited the victory of the nobility over the common people.* At Rome, Jugurtha had regarded him as an opponent, but now treated him with meticulous respect, and by lavish gifts and promises induced him to set Jugurtha's advantage before reputation and honour – indeed, before all his own true interests. Jugurtha went to work on similar lines with the other members of the commission and got most of them on his side. Only a few were above being bought. In the division of territory, the part of Numidia adjoining Mauretania – the more fertile and more thickly populated part – was assigned to Jugurtha. The share that fell to Adherbal might have looked like a better bargain, because it had more harbours and buildings, but its real value was less.†

It seems to me appropriate at this point to give a short account of the geography of Africa, and to mention briefly the peoples of that continent with whom we have fought or contracted alliances. Concerning those regions and tribes which are seldom visited because the country is hot or mountainous or desert, I am not in a position to give any reliable information; and the rest I shall deal with in the fewest possible words.

In mapping out the earth's surface most authorities recognize Africa as a third continent, though a few admit only Asia and Europe as continents, including Africa in Europe. Africa is bounded on the west by the strait which lies between our sea and the Ocean;‡ on the east, by the broad sloping plateau

* See Introduction, p. 24.

† This is Roman propaganda: Jugurtha's share was certainly the less valuable.

‡ The Straits of Gibraltar.

which its inhabitants call Catabathmos.* The sea that washes the coast is dangerous, and there are few harbours. The soil produces good crops of grain and good pasture, but is unsuitable for the cultivation of trees. The rainfall is very low, and rivers and springs few and far between. The natives are healthy, active, and capable of hard toil. Death by disease is rare: most of them die of old age, except those who are killed by enemies or by the savage wild beasts with which the country abounds.

I will now describe very briefly the aborigines of Africa, the immigrant races, and the cross-breeding that took place. My account differs from the common tradition on the subject: it is based on a translation supplied to me of some books in the Carthaginian language, attributed to King Hiempsal,† and it agrees with the beliefs of the Africans themselves. My authorities must take the responsibility for its accuracy.

Africa was originally inhabited by the Gaetulians and Libyans – barbarous, uncivilized people who lived on the flesh of wild animals or, like cattle, on the grass of the field.‡ Without recognized customs or laws, they obeyed no ruler, but lived a nomadic life, roaming from place to place and bivouacking wherever they happened to be at nightfall. When Hercules died in Spain – as the Africans believe he did – his army, composed of various nationalities, was left without a leader; and since each contingent claimed the right to choose new commanders, the whole force soon broke up. The Medes, Persians, and Armenians sailed across to Africa and settled on the Mediterranean coast.§ The Persians went to the extreme

* The plateau lying between Cyrenaica and Egypt.

† Not the cousin of Jugurtha, but the son of his half-brother Gauda who is mentioned in section 65.

‡ The Gaetulians and Libyans, who formed the chief element in the Numidian population, belonged to the race from which the modern Kabyles or Berbers are descended.

§ The story of these Medes, Persians, and Armenians, who were brought by Hercules to Spain and afterwards crossed to Africa, may recall early migrations of Aryan people across the Straits of Gibraltar.

west, close to the Atlantic seaboard, where they lived in cabins made by turning the hulls of their ships upside-down. For there was no timber in that country, nor could they obtain it from the Spaniards by purchase or barter, as the wide stretch of sea intervening and their ignorance of the language made trading impossible. By intermarriage they gradually coalesced with the Gaetulians; and since their constant search for suitable land kept them on the move from one place to another, they called themselves Nomads. To this day the dwellings of the Numidian peasants, which are called *mapalia*, are long and narrow, with sides curving overhead to form roofs, like the ribs of a ship. The Medes and Armenians were joined by the Libyans – who lived closer to the African sea, whereas the Gaetulians were farther south, not far from the torrid zone – and these peoples soon possessed towns: for being separated from Spain only by a narrow strait, they had instituted a system of barter with that country. The name of the Medes was in course of time altered by the Libyans, who in their barbarous tongue substituted the form *Mauri*.* The power of the Persians and Gaetulians soon increased, and at a later date a section of them separated from the parent stock on account of over-population, and under the name of Numidians occupied the district bordering on Carthage which is now called Numidia. The parent state and its offshoot gave each other mutual support, which enabled them to conquer or overawe their neighbours and to win great renown – especially the section which had advanced to the Mediterranean: for the Libyans were unwarlike in comparison with the Gaetulians. Eventually, the greater part of the coastal area fell into the hands of the Numidians, and all the conquered peoples were merged in the conquering race and took its name.

In later times came Phoenicians, who, either to relieve

* i.e. Moors, the inhabitants of the country then called Mauretania. This derivation of *Mauri* is, of course, a fanciful one.

over-population at home or from a desire for conquest, had induced men of the lower classes and others who were eager for adventure to emigrate. They founded Hippo, Hadrumetum, Leptis,* and other cities on the coast, which soon became so prosperous that they could protect the interests or enhance the prestige of their mother-country. Of Carthage I will give no description: for I think it better to say nothing than to offer an inadequate account, and it is time I passed on to other topics.

Starting at Catabathmos, which divides Egypt from Africa, and following the coast,† you come first to Cyrene, a colony founded from Thera; next to the two Syrtes, with Leptis between them; and then to the Altars of the Philaeni, which the Carthaginians regarded as the frontier of their empire in the direction of Egypt, and to other Punic towns. The rest of the land, as far west as Mauretania, is held by the Numidians. Nearest to Spain are the Moors. South of Numidia, we are told, are the Gaetulians, some of whom live in huts while others are uncivilized nomads. Farther still to the south are the Ethiopians, beyond whom are lands parched by the continual heat of the sun.

At the outbreak of the war with Jugurtha, most of the Punic towns, in addition to the territory held by Carthage immediately before her destruction, were administered by Roman governors. A considerable part of the country inhabited by

* Hippo may be either Hippo Regius, which was near the place where Bône is now, or Hippo Zarytus (Bizerta). Hadrumetum was on the east coast of Tunis (now Susa). Leptis is probably Leptis Minor, a short distance south of Hadrumetum.

† The geography is confused. Cyrene was an important Greek colony on the coast of Cyrenaica; it was founded about 630 B.C. from the island of Thera (now Santorin) in the Aegean Sea. The Greater Syrtis is the Gulf of Sidra, immediately to the west of Cyrenaica. Leptis is Leptis Magna (modern Lebda), the easternmost of the three cities of Tripolitania. The Lesser Syrtis is the Gulf of Gabès on the coast of Tunisia. On the Altars of the Philaeni, see below, section 79.

the Gaetulians, as well as Numidia right up to its western boundary the River Muluccha,* was subject to Jugurtha. The Moors were all ruled over by King Bocchus, who knew the Roman people only by name, and was at that time equally unknown to us either as friend or foe. That is all I need say about Africa and its inhabitants.

After the partition of the Numidian kingdom the Roman commission left Africa. Jugurtha, finding that his fears had been groundless and that he had attained the object for which his crime had been committed, was convinced that his friends at Numantia had spoken no more than the truth when they told him that everything at Rome had its price; and his ambitious hopes were further encouraged by the promises of the men whose avarice he had so recently glutted with his presents. So he began to cast his eyes on Adherbal's kingdom. Jugurtha was energetic and warlike, while his intended victim was quiet and peace-loving, of a meek disposition that seemed to invite attack, and too timid to inspire fear. Accordingly, Jugurtha suddenly invaded his territory with a large force, taking many prisoners as well as cattle and other plunder, setting fire to buildings, and making cavalry raids in various places.† He then retreated with all his men into his own kingdom, assuming that Adherbal's resentment at this aggression would tempt him to counter-attack, which would give Jugurtha a pretext for making open war upon him. But Adherbal, who now realized that he was no match for his enemy in the field, and had more confidence in the Roman alliance than in his Numidians, merely sent ambassadors to Jugurtha to protest against the outrage; and although insults were all he got by way of answer, he determined to put up with anything rather than

* The River Muluccha is the Moulouya, the boundary between Algeria and Morocco.

† This invasion took place in 113 B.C., three years after the division of the kingdom. Sallust speaks as if it had followed almost immediately.

resort to war, after the failure of his first attempt. This forbearance, however, did nothing to restrain the ambition of Jugurtha, who already imagined himself as master of the whole of Adherbal's kingdom. He took the field, therefore, not as before with a band of marauders, but at the head of a large army that he had raised, and openly sought to make himself ruler of all Numidia. Wherever he marched he laid waste towns and countryside and drove off the animals as booty, inspiring his own troops with fresh courage and his enemy with increased terror.

Adherbal now realized things had gone so far that he must either abandon his kingdom altogether or hold it by force of arms. Much against his will, therefore, he mustered an army and advanced against Jugurtha. Both armies encamped for the time being near the town of Cirta,* not far from the sea. They did not engage that day, because it was too late; but in the early hours of the morning, while it was still fairly dark, Jugurtha's men were given the signal to assault the enemy's camp, and surprising them while they were half asleep or in the act of seizing their arms, routed them completely. Adherbal fled with a few horsemen to Cirta; and had it not been for a crowd of Italian civilians, who prevented his pursuers from entering the town, a single day would have seen the beginning and the end of the war between the two kings. As it was, Jugurtha invested the town and attempted to storm it by means of mantlets, siege-towers, and machines of every description – the object of this extreme haste being to secure a *fait accompli* before the return of the embassy which he knew Adherbal had dispatched to Rome before the battle.

However, when the Senate heard that the kings were at war, a deputation of three young men was sent to Africa with instructions to approach them both and to inform them that

* This city – the modern Constantine – was an important centre of the grain trade. Hence the number of Italians resident there.

it was the desire and recommendation of the Roman Senate and People that they should lay down their arms; this – they were to say – was the course consistent with their own honour and the honour of Rome. The deputies soon arrived in Africa, making the more haste because, just as they were preparing to start, reports reached Rome of the battle that had taken place and of the siege of Cirta – though these reports favoured Jugurtha by understating the facts. After listening to their address, Jugurtha replied that there was nothing to which he attached more weight or for which he had greater respect than the opinion of the Senate. From his youth, he said, he had made every effort to earn the approval of all good patriots. It was his merits – not the sort of villainy with which his enemies charged him – that had endeared him to the great Publius Scipio; and it was the same good qualities, and not any lack of children of his own, that persuaded Micipsa to adopt him as joint heir to his kingdom. Having always done his duty as an honest man, he was the less disposed to submit to wrong. Adherbal had treacherously conspired to take his life, and on discovering this wicked plot he had taken measures to prevent its execution. It would not be right or just for Rome to deny him the rights to which the law of nations entitled him. After he had added that he would shortly send an embassy to Rome to explain the whole situation, the interview came to an end. The deputies had no opportunity of making representations to Adherbal.

Jugurtha waited till he thought they would have left Africa, and then, since its natural strength prevented his taking Cirta by storm, surrounded the walls with a palisade and trench, erected and manned siege-towers, and pressed his attack day and night by open force and by stratagem. He used both promises and threats to undermine the allegiance of the defenders, and harangues to raise the morale of his own troops, omitting nothing that determination and energy could do.

Adherbal saw that he was in a desperate position – assailed by an enemy bent on his destruction, without hope of succour, and unable to prolong the struggle because he lacked supplies. So, choosing two of the bravest of the men who had fled with him to Cirta, he persuaded them, by making liberal promises and by dwelling on his pitiful plight, to make their way through the enemy's lines to the nearest point on the coast, and from there to Rome.

These Numidians accomplished their journey in the course of a few days, and Adherbal's letter was read to the Senate. Its substance was as follows:

'Members of the Senate, it is no fault of mine that I have to appeal to you once more. I am compelled to do so by the violent conduct of Jugurtha, who is so bent on destroying me that he has no respect either for you or for the gods, and thirsts for my blood above everything else. So for more than four months I have been besieged by his army, and it avails me nothing that I am a friend and ally of the Roman people, that my father Micipsa did so much for Jugurtha, and that you have passed decrees in my favour: sword and hunger alike harass me, and it would be hard to say which is the worse.

'I will not say more about Jugurtha. The sorry plight to which I have been brought is proof that it would be useless: I have found by experience that the complaints of the unfortunate are not taken seriously. It is plain, however, that he is aiming at something more than my downfall. He cannot hope to obtain my kingdom and at the same time keep your friendship; and which of the two he sets more store by, no one can fail to see, since he began by murdering my brother Hiempsal and then drove me from the kingdom of my fathers. The extent of the wrongs suffered personally by me and my brother is no concern of yours. But now he is in armed occupation of a kingdom that belongs to you, and is keeping me, whom you placed on the throne of Numidia, shut up in Cirta. How much notice he takes of the warnings of your ambassadors, my parlous condition shows. What is there left that can influence him, save only the force that you can bring to bear on him? I only wish that the words I am now writing, as well as my earlier protests in the Senate, were false – that my miseries did not prove what I say to be only too true. But since it seems as if I had been born for no other purpose than to show what wickedness Jugurtha is capable of, I no longer ask to escape sorrow or death, but only to be spared the physical tortures I shall have to endure if I fall into my enemy's power. The kingdom of Numidia is yours, and you can do with it what you please. But save me from his godless hands, I implore you by the majesty of your imperial sway and by the sacred rights of friendship, if you still retain any memories of my grandfather Masinissa.'

When the letter had been read, some proposed that an army should be sent to Africa to rescue Adherbal with all speed and that in the meantime the Senate should discuss what was to be done to Jugurtha for his failure to obey the commissioners. But the group of senators who were always on the king's side, by making extraordinary efforts, prevented the passing of a decree to this effect, so that the public good, as so often happens, was sacrificed to private interests. However, a commission was appointed to go to Africa, consisting this time of men of mature years and noble birth who had held high office; it included the Marcus Scaurus whom I mentioned previously, an ex-consul and at that time leader of the House. On account of the public indignation the affair had aroused, as well as the urgent entreaties of the Numidian envoys, the commissioners embarked within three days, and after a quick passage to Utica* sent a letter to Jugurtha calling upon him to present himself in the Roman Province immediately, as they were deputed by

* The capital of the Roman Province of Africa, situated a little to the north of Carthage.

the Senate to interview him. The news that men of standing, who were said to have great power in Rome, had come to hinder his designs was a shock to Jugurtha. At first he was torn between fear and desire, dreading the Senate's anger if he disobeyed its agents, but at the same time tempted by blind passion to continue his career of crime. But covetousness soon prevailed, and he chose the evil course. Accordingly he surrounded Cirta with his army and made a supreme effort to break his way in, hoping that the division of the enemy's forces might give him a chance of succeeding either by force or by stratagem. However, he had to give it up as a bad job; and since he could not now hope to get Adherbal into his power before going to meet the commissioners, and feared that further delay might anger Scaurus, of whom he was most afraid, he entered the Province with a small escort of cavalry. The commissioners warned him of the severe punishment that the Senate would mete out for his refusal to raise the siege, but all their eloquence was wasted, and they had to leave without obtaining any concession from him.

When they heard about this in Cirta, the Italians whose brave defence had so far saved the town felt that they could now safely capitulate, as the great prestige of Rome would protect them from injury. So they advised Adherbal to surrender himself and the town to Jugurtha, merely stipulating that his life should be spared; everything else, they said, the Senate would see to. To trust Jugurtha's word was the last thing Adherbal would have chosen to do, but it was no good his refusing, since they were in a position to force his hand. So he took their advice and surrendered. Jugurtha's first act was to torture him to death. Then he put to the sword all the adult men who were found with arms in their possession, making no distinction between Numidians and foreign traders.

CHAPTER V

THE FIRST CAMPAIGNS (111–109 B.C.)

IN due course the news reached Rome and the matter came up for discussion in the Senate. Jugurtha's cat's-paws kept interrupting the debate and spinning it out by making appeals to friends and wrangling with opponents, seeking by every means to minimize the enormity of his deed. And had not Gaius Memmius, an energetic man who always opposed the power of the nobility and was at the time tribune elect, made the people understand that the object of this small group of intriguers was to enable the guilty king to go scot-free, the discussions would undoubtedly have dragged on until all public resentment had evaporated; such was the power of the king's influence and money. However, the Senate had a guilty conscience and feared the people. So in accordance with the provisions of the Sempronian law,* Numidia and Italy were assigned as their provinces to the consuls about to be elected.† The candidates returned were Publius Scipio Nasica, to whom Italy was allotted, and Lucius Calpurnius Bestia, who received Numidia. Troops were then enrolled for service in Africa, and money was voted for the men's pay and other military requirements.

Jugurtha was taken aback by these developments, for he had it firmly fixed in his mind that there was nothing money could not do at Rome. He sent his son and two close friends as a deputation to the Senate, instructing them, as he had done after the assassination of Hiempsal, to offer bribes to everyone

* A law of Gaius Gracchus providing that every year, before the consular elections, the Senate should designate two provinces as consular provinces; during their term of office the consuls decided, by agreement or by casting lots, which of the two provinces each should take.

† For the year 111.

they met. When they were approaching Rome, Bestia asked the Senate whether it was its pleasure to admit the envoys into the city, and the House decreed that unless they came to make unconditional surrender of Jugurtha and his kingdom they were to leave Italy within ten days. The consul caused them to be notified of the Senate's decision, and they had to return home with their object unaccomplished.

Bestia, who had now levied his army, chose as members of his staff a number of noblemen, good party men whose support he hoped would countenance any misconduct of his own – including Scaurus, whose character and habits I have already described. For although the consul had many good qualities of mind and body, they were all rendered useless by his avarice. He had great power of endurance and a keen and far-seeing intellect; no novice in the art of war, he showed admirable courage in facing perils and the attacks of personal enemies. The legions marched overland to Reggio and were conveyed thence first to Sicily and then to Africa.

After organizing his commissariat, Bestia began operations with a swift invasion of Numidia, taking many prisoners and capturing several towns by assault. Then, however, Jugurtha sent agents who tempted him by offers of money and warned him that he had a difficult war on hand. Demoralized as he was by covetousness, he quickly succumbed, and took Scaurus as his accomplice to help him in his designs. Scaurus had vigorously opposed Jugurtha at first, when most of the other members of his party had been corrupted; but an enormous bribe had now seduced him from the path of virtue. At first Jugurtha tried merely to bargain for a suspension of hostilities, thinking that this would give him time to arrange something at Rome by bribery or influence. But when he knew that Scaurus was taking a hand in the business, he felt confident that he would be able to obtain peace terms and decided to open negotiations in person with the Roman commanders. As a token of good faith the consul sent his quaestor Sextius to Vaga,* one of Jugurtha's towns – ostensibly to take delivery of the grain which he had openly demanded from the king's envoys in return for observing an armistice until terms of surrender could be arranged. Thereupon Jugurtha, in pursuance of his plan, went to the Roman camp. In a short statement before the council of war he complained of the unfair construction put upon his actions and asked to be allowed to surrender; but all the details he arranged privately with Bestia and Scaurus. On the following day the terms were submitted *en bloc* to a vote of the council and the offer of surrender was accepted. In accordance with the demands made in the presence of the council, thirty elephants and a large number of cattle and horses, as well as a small amount of silver, were handed over to the quaestor. Bestia then set out for Rome to preside over the elections, and the Numidians and our army lived for the time being on a peaceful footing.

When reports reached Rome of the events in Africa and of the manner in which they had been brought about, the consul's conduct was discussed wherever people met together. The masses were gravely incensed against him, while the senators were filled with anxiety. Should they endorse such a disgraceful act or should they annul the consul's decree? They could not make up their minds. It was chiefly the power of Scaurus, who was reported to be the prompter and accomplice of Bestia, that deterred them from taking the honest and patriotic course. But while the Senate hesitated and stalled, Gaius Memmius, whose independent character and hatred of the privileges of the nobility have already been mentioned, kept on addressing meetings of citizens and urging them to take vengeance on the guilty and to be true to the Republic and to their own liberties. Setting forth the many arrogant and cruel acts of the nobles, he did his utmost to inflame the

* The modern Beja, about sixty miles west of Tunis.

people's feelings. Since in this period Memmius's eloquence was famous at Rome and exercised much influence, I have thought it appropriate to reproduce one of his many speeches in full, and I have chosen the one which he delivered in a public meeting after Bestia's return. It ran somewhat as follows:

'There are many reasons, fellow citizens, which would deter me from interesting myself on your behalf, were it not that my concern for our country outweighs every other consideration. Rome is saddled with a powerful oligarchy to which you tamely submit; your legal rights are denied you; worst of all, uprightness is more likely to endanger a man than to add to his credit. I hate having to remind you how for the past fifteen years you have been made the sport of an arrogant ruling class; how your champions have been shamefully done to death with none to avenge them; how your spirit is so demoralized by cowardice and sloth that even now when your enemies are at your mercy you do not rise against them, but still fear men who ought to fear you. Yet in spite of all this, my heart prompts me to resist the tyranny of this faction. I mean to exercise that right of free speech which I inherited from my father – though whether it will do any good or not depends on you, my friends. I do not urge you to take up arms against your oppressors, as your ancestors often did. There is no need to use force, no need to rend the state asunder: let their own wickedness destroy them. After the murder of Tiberius Gracchus, who was alleged to be aspiring to royal power, prosecutions were instituted against the common people of Rome.* Again, after Gaius Gracchus and Marcus Fulvius Flaccus had been assassinated, many of your fellow commoners were done to death in prison;† and in both cases it was not the law, but the killers' good pleasure, that ended the bloodshed. Well, for the sake of argument let us grant that an attempt to restore their rights to the people was a bid for monarchical

* See Introduction, p. 21. † See Introduction, p. 24.

power, and that the acts of terrorism which followed – since they cannot be avenged without more shedding of citizens' blood – were legitimate. But for many years you had to watch in silent indignation while the treasury was pillaged, while kings and free peoples paid tribute for the benefit of a clique of noblemen who monopolized all honour and wealth. Not content with committing such crimes with impunity, they have gone further: your laws, your national honour, every obligation owed to god or man, have now been betrayed to the enemies of your country. And the men who have done these deeds show neither shame nor contrition, but strut proudly before your faces flaunting their priesthoods and consulships, and some of them their triumphal honours, as if these things were prizes they had deserved and not spoils that they have seized. Even slaves who are bought and sold refuse to endure unjust treatment from their masters: will you who were born to rule submit patiently to servitude?

'But what manner of men are they who have made themselves rulers of the state? They are evildoers whose hands are red with blood. Covetous beyond measure and stained with guilt, they are none the less swollen with pride, and there is nothing that they will not sell: honour, reputation, natural affection, every virtue indeed – as well as every vice – is to them a source of profit. They have murdered your tribunes, condemned innocent men on trumped-up charges, and shed your blood – all to secure their own position. Thus the worse crimes they commit the more unassailable they become, and instead of living in fear lest their wickedness be punished, they take advantage of your faintheartedness to make *you* afraid. Sharing as they all do the same desires, hatreds, and fears, they stick closely together; if they were honest men, you could call it friendship: but these are just a gang of criminals. If your love of liberty were as ardent as their craving for power, our country would surely not be violated as she now is, and your electoral favours would be bestowed on the most deserving citizens, instead of on the most shameless. Your ancestors, in order to assert their rights and vindicate the status of the commons, twice left the city with arms in their hands and occupied the Aventine hill.* And will you not strain every nerve to defend the freedom which they bequeathed to you – and indeed with all the greater vigour inasmuch as it is a greater dishonour to lose that which has once been won than never to have won it?

'"What then do you suggest?" someone will ask. "Are we to punish those who have betrayed the Republic to its enemy?" Not, I answer, by the use of violence – which would ill become you, even if they deserve it – but by prosecutions in the law-courts, where Jugurtha himself can be called on to give evidence. For if his surrender means anything, he surely will not fail to obey your commands. If he disregards them, you can judge for yourselves what kind of peace and what kind of surrender it is by which he obtains impunity for his crimes and a few powerful men become immensely rich, while the state gets nothing but loss and disgrace. Are you not even yet sick of their tyranny? Would you like to bring back those days when kingdoms, provinces, laws, privileges, law-courts, decisions about war and peace – everything you possessed, in short – were in the control of a handful of men, while you, the people of Rome, whom no enemy could conquer and all nations obeyed, were content if you were graciously permitted to remain alive? For as to enslavement, who among you had the courage to resist it?

'For my own part, although I think that for a true man it is the lowest depth of shame to submit tamely to wrongs, I

* According to tradition there were several of these 'secessions of the plebs' during the early Republican period. The common people retired outside the city boundary, thus not only going on strike but withdrawing themselves for the time being from the life of the community.

should have no objection to your pardoning these wicked men, since they are your fellow citizens, were it not that such mercy would end in your ruin. For in their outrageous insolence they will not be content with impunity for past offences: you must wrest from them the power of offending in future. Otherwise, you will live in everlasting anxiety: for you will find that you must either accept slavery or fight to preserve your freedom. What hope can there be of mutual trust or union between you and them? They want to rule, you want to be free; they, to do you wrong, you, to prevent them. Moreover, they treat our allies as enemies and our enemies as allies. Where there is such divergence of purposes, can peace or friendship exist?

'I strongly advise you, therefore, not to let this atrocious crime go unpunished. This is not a matter of defrauding the public treasury or extorting money from provincials – offences to which, serious though they are, we have become so accustomed that we count them as nothing. Our bitterest foe has had the authority of the Senate and your sovereign power delivered into his hands. In Rome, as well as at the battle front, the Republic has been put up for sale. Unless those responsible for these outrages are brought to trial and punished, we must live in bondage to tyrants. For if a man can do whatever he pleases with impunity, what is he but a despot?

'The last thing I would suggest is that you should derive any satisfaction from fellow-citizens' misdeeds. But do not, by pardoning wrongdoers, go the way to ruin innocent men. In politics it is much better to leave a service unrecompensed than to let an injury go unpunished. For a good man merely becomes less active in well-doing when no notice is taken of him; a bad man becomes worse than he was before. And the prevention of wrongdoing is the important thing: for then people will not often stand in need of protection.'

By repeating these and similar arguments, Memmius

persuaded the people to send the praetor Lucius Cassius* to Jugurtha with instructions to bring him to Rome under a safe-conduct, so that his testimony could furnish proof against Scaurus and the others whom Memmius intended to prosecute for receiving bribes. Meanwhile, the officers whom Bestia had left in charge of the army in Numidia, following their commander's example, were guilty of many scandalous misdeeds. Some of them were induced by bribes to return Jugurtha's elephants to him, some sold back the deserters, while others plundered people with whom Rome was no longer at war. So virulent was the epidemic of greed that had attacked them. When Memmius carried his motion, to the general consternation of the nobility, Cassius went to meet Jugurtha. The king was frightened and in a pessimistic mood because he knew he was guilty; and Cassius persuaded him that since he had surrendered to the Romans he would do better to throw himself on their mercy than to risk provoking their anger. Cassius confirmed the official pledge of immunity by his own personal undertaking, which in view of his high reputation at that time Jugurtha considered equally valuable.

Accordingly the king, after putting on mourning in order to excite pity by the striking contrast with his customary royal attire, accompanied Cassius to Rome. Although he had plenty of personal courage and determination, and was supported by all those whose power or wickedness had enabled him to do so much, he nevertheless paid a large sum to secure the services of a shameless tribune named Gaius Baebius, which he hoped would protect him against either prosecution or illegal violence. When Memmius summoned a meeting of citizens, the common people showed bitter hostility to Jugurtha, some demanding that he should be imprisoned, others

* Lucius Cassius Longinus, praetor 111 B.C., consul (with Marius) 107. During his consulship he was killed fighting in Gaul against the Celtic tribe of the Tigurini, which had joined forces with the invading Cimbri.

that if he would not reveal the names of his accomplices he should be executed as an enemy of the state, in accordance with traditional usage. But Memmius, who had more regard for Roman honour than for their anger, tried to calm their excited feelings, declaring that he would not do anything to encourage a violation of Rome's plighted word. Finally, when he had obtained silence, he brought Jugurtha forward and taxed him with his conduct at Rome and in Numidia and with the crimes he had committed against his father and brothers. He said that although the Roman people knew who had been his tools and abettors in all this, they wished to have a clearer statement from his own lips. If he would reveal the truth, he could put his trust in the good faith and clemency of Rome; if he refused to speak, he would do his accomplices no good and could hope for no mercy for himself.

When Memmius had finished speaking Jugurtha was called on to reply, but Gaius Baebius, the tribune whom he had bought, bade him hold his peace. And in spite of the furious indignation of the crowd, which tried to intimidate the tribune with shouts and hostile looks, sometimes even with threatening gestures and all the other menaces that angry men indulge in, he was not to be deterred from his shameless course. Their will thus contemptuously thwarted, the people departed, and Jugurtha, Bestia, and their supporters, who had been much perturbed at the prospect of an inquiry, recovered their hardihood.

There was in Rome at the time a Numidian called Massiva, a son of Gulussa and grandson of Masinissa. Because he had taken sides against Jugurtha in the dynastic struggle, he had fled from Numidia after the surrender of Cirta and the murder of Adherbal. This man was persuaded by Spurius Albinus, who with Quintus Minucius Rufus was consul the year after Bestia,* to claim the Numidian throne from the

* i.e. 110 B.C.

Senate, pointing out that he was descended from Masinissa, and that Jugurtha by his crimes had made himself an object of hatred and fear. Albinus was eager to conduct a war, and therefore wanted to keep everything in a state of turmoil and not allow public interest to subside. He had been allotted the province of Numidia, while Minucius had obtained Macedonia. When Massiva started intriguing to achieve his purpose, Jugurtha got little help from his partisans: some of them were embarrassed by consciousness of guilt, while others were in such bad odour with the people that they dared not stir in the matter. So he had recourse once more to the power of money, which he had used so often with success. Sending for Bomilcar, his most intimate and devoted attendant, he told him to hire assassins to attack Massiva – secretly, if it could possibly be managed; if not, he must kill him as best he could. Bomilcar lost no time in executing the king's commands. Employing men who were experts in such business, he got information about Massiva's comings and goings, so that he knew where he was likely to be found at any time. When circumstances were favourable an ambush was laid. One of the assassins who had been engaged attacked Massiva rather incautiously. He killed his man, but got caught, and was persuaded by the consul Albinus and a number of others to turn informer. Bomilcar was put on trial – a prosecution which served the ends of justice and morality, but was not strictly in accordance with the law of nations, since he was a member of the suite of a man who had come to Rome under protection of an official safe-conduct. In spite of his obvious guilt, Jugurtha persisted in denying the evidence which connected him with this heinous crime until he saw that the indignation it had aroused was too great to be bought off by money or influence. At Bomilcar's first appearance in court Jugurtha had offered fifty members of his suite as sureties; but being more concerned about his throne than about the sureties, and fearing that if Bomilcar was put to death the rest of his subjects would be too frightened to obey him in future, he smuggled him away to Numidia. A few days later he himself was ordered by the Senate to leave Italy, and set out for home. After passing through the gates of Rome, it is said that he looked back at the city several times in silence, and finally exclaimed: 'Yonder is a city put up for sale, and its days are numbered if it finds a buyer.'

The war was then resumed. Albinus hastily transported to Africa provisions, money for paying the troops, and other essential supplies, and set out at once himself. The elections were due shortly, and he was anxious to bring hostilities to an end before then, whether by victory in the field or by inducing Jugurtha to surrender or by any other means. Jugurtha, however, did all he could to gain time, and continually invented fresh ways of delaying matters – promising to surrender and then pretending to fear double-dealing, retreating before Albinus's attack and almost immediately counter-attacking to encourage his troops. Thus all the consul's efforts were foiled: he could neither get on with the war nor obtain peace. Some people thought at the time that he must have known quite well what Jugurtha's plan was. After starting operations with such energetic haste, he had made little effort to prevent their being brought to a standstill, and it seemed unthinkable that this could be due merely to indolence: it looked more like treachery. In any case, time was allowed to slip by until the day of the elections was now close at hand, whereupon Albinus set sail for Italy, leaving his brother Aulus in the camp as acting praetor.

In Rome, meanwhile, serious disturbances were resulting from civil strife fomented by the tribunes, two of whom, Publius Lucullus and Lucius Annius, were trying in spite of their colleagues' opposition to get themselves elected to a further term of office. This dispute prevented the holding of elections all that year, and extended the period during which

Aulus Albinus was left as acting praetor in charge of his brother's camp. He thought he saw an opportunity of either bringing the war to an end or extorting money out of Jugurtha by threatening him with an offensive. During January* he summoned his troops from their winter quarters for active service, and by forced marches in severe wintry weather reached the town of Suthul,† where the king's treasure was kept. The bad weather and the natural strength of the place made it impossible either to storm it or to lay siege to it; for all round the walls, which were built on the edge of a precipitous cliff, lay a swampy plain which had been turned by the winter rains into a lake. Yet Aulus, either with the purpose of frightening Jugurtha by a feint, or blinded by his eagerness to gain the town for the sake of its treasure, brought up mantlets, raised a siege-terrace, and pushed forward with other preparations for an attack.

Jugurtha was well aware that Aulus was a conceited ignoramus, and craftily encouraged his folly, sending a succession of envoys to beg humbly for terms of surrender, while he himself pretended to be afraid to come near and led his army along paths traversing wooded hills. Eventually, by holding out hope of an agreement, he induced the Roman to raise the siege of Suthul and follow him in his feigned retreat into secluded country where – as he pointed out – the treason which Aulus contemplated could be more easily concealed. Meanwhile he was employing skilful agents who worked day and night to corrupt the Roman army, bribing centurions and cavalry officers either to desert or to abandon their posts at a given signal. When all had been arranged to his satisfaction, at dead of night he suddenly surrounded the camp with a host of Numidians. The Romans were disconcerted by this sudden

* 109 B.C.

† A site not certainly identified, but probably near Guelma, some thirty-five miles south-west of Bône.

alarm and ran excitedly about the camp, seizing their arms, trying to hide, or reassuring their frightened comrades. The enemy were there in great strength, the darkness of night was intensified by clouds, and whatever course they took was fraught with danger: no one could tell whether it was safer to flee or to stay where they were. Then the men who were in Jugurtha's pay took a hand. One cohort of Ligurians and two squadrons of Thracian cavalry, with a handful of Roman privates, deserted to the king, while the chief centurion of the third legion allowed the enemy to break in through the section of the rampart which he had been appointed to defend. Here the Numidians burst in *en masse*, and our men disgraced themselves by fleeing – most of them even throwing down their arms – and took refuge on a nearby hill. The darkness, and the delay occasioned by their stopping to plunder the camp, prevented the enemy from exploiting their victory. On the following day, in a conference with Aulus, Jugurtha pointed out that he had him and his army surrounded, and could either put them to the sword or starve them to death; however – since no man could be sure that he would not one day find himself in a like case – if Aulus would make a treaty with him, he would spare all their lives and content himself with making them pass under a yoke in token of surrender, provided that they evacuated Numidia within ten days. Hard and humiliating as these conditions were, men who had the fear of death before their eyes had no choice but to accept whatever terms the king was pleased to offer.

When news of the disaster reached Rome, the city was overcome by grief and fear. Some mourned for the glory of their empire, others, in their ignorance of warfare, were afraid for their liberty. All were bitter against Aulus – especially those who had had distinguished military careers – for submitting to such a disgrace when his men had weapons in their hands, instead of making them fight their way to safety. The consul Albinus, fearing that the indignation aroused by his brother's misconduct would eventually prove dangerous, took steps to submit the question of the treaty to the Senate. Without waiting for the Senate's decision, however, he proceeded to enrol reinforcements, recruited auxiliary contingents from the Italian allies and communities possessing 'Latin' rights,* and busied himself generally. The Senate very properly decided that without its consent and that of the Roman people no agreement that had been made could have the force of a treaty. Albinus, although he was prevented by a veto of the tribunes from taking with him the forces he had raised, himself started for Africa in the course of a few days; for the whole of the original army, after evacuating Numidia in accordance with the agreement, was wintering in the Roman Province. He arrived there eagerly anxious to prosecute the war against Jugurtha and so dispel the odium his brother had incurred; but when he found what a state the troops were in – demoralized not only by their rout but by the licence and indulgence resulting from relaxation of discipline – he decided that he was not in a position to make any move at the moment.

In Rome, meanwhile, a tribune named Gaius Mamilius Limetanus proposed a bill directing criminal proceedings to be instituted against persons who had instigated Jugurtha to defy the Senate's decrees or had accepted presents of money from him while serving as envoys or commanders, as well as against those who restored to Jugurtha his elephants and deserters and those who had made agreements with the enemy concerning war and peace. This proposal alarmed both those

* At this date the great majority of Italian communities did not possess Roman citizenship. But some of them had special privileges, including the right to make commercial contracts with Romans and to contract legal marriages with Roman women, and the right to acquire Roman citizenship by holding office in their own townships. These were called 'Latin' rights because they had been granted first to ancient towns in Latium such as Tibur (Tivoli) and Praeneste (Palestrina).

who knew themselves to be guilty and others who feared prosecution because they were hated by the democrats. But they could not openly oppose it without admitting their approval of the kind of acts it sought to punish. So they went to work secretly, employing various acquaintances – particularly men from 'Latin' and other Italian towns – to obstruct its passage. But the populace showed incredible eagerness and determination in passing the bill into law – more from hatred of the nobility, against whom these severe measures were directed, than from patriotism; so high did political passions run. Amid the exultation of the people and the panic of his dismayed friends, Marcus Scaurus, whom I have mentioned as having been one of Bestia's lieutenants, took advantage of the continuing confusion in the city to get himself appointed one of the three special judges whom the new law required to be chosen by the people. The investigation, however, was conducted harshly and oppressively, on hearsay evidence, and according to the caprice of the mob. The nobles had played the tyrant often enough in the past; but now the proletariat was on top and showed itself as arrogant as they had been.

The division of the Roman state into warring factions, with all its attendant vices, had originated some years before, as a result of peace and of that material prosperity which men regard as the greatest blessing. Down to the destruction of Carthage,* the people and Senate shared the government peaceably and with due restraint, and the citizens did not compete for glory or power; fear of its enemies preserved the good morals of the state. But when the people were relieved of this fear, the favourite vices of prosperity – licence and pride – appeared as a natural consequence. Thus the peace and quiet which they had longed for in time of adversity proved, when they obtained it, to be even more grievous and bitter than the adversity. For the nobles started to use their position, and the

* 146 B.C.

people their liberty, to gratify their selfish passions, every man snatching and seizing what he could for himself. So the whole community was split into parties, and the Republic, which hitherto had been the common interest of all, was torn asunder. The nobility had the advantage of being a close-knit body, whereas the democratic party was weakened by its loose organization, its supporters being dispersed among a huge multitude. One small group of oligarchs had everything in its control alike in peace and war – the treasury, the provinces, public offices, all distinctions and triumphs. The people were burdened with military service and poverty, while the spoils of war were snatched by the generals and shared with a handful of friends. Meantime, the soldiers' parents or young children, if they happened to have a powerful neighbour, might well be driven from their homes. Thus the possession of power gave unlimited scope to ruthless greed, which violated and plundered everything, respecting nothing and holding nothing sacred, till finally it brought about its own downfall. For the day came when noblemen rose to power who preferred true glory to unjust dominion: then the state was shaken to its foundations by civil strife, as by an earthquake.

So when Tiberius and Gaius Gracchus,* men whose ancestors had done much in the Punic and other wars to increase the power of Rome, sought to establish the liberty of the common people and expose the crimes of the oligarchs, the guilty nobles took fright and opposed their proceedings by every means at their disposal, using now the Italian allies and 'Latin' communities, now the Equestrian Order, whom they had seduced from the people's cause by holding out to them the hope of being allowed to share their own privileges. First Tiberius was butchered when he was actually a tribune; a few years later – because he tried to follow in his brother's footsteps – Gaius suffered the same fate when he was a member of the

* See Introduction, pp. 20–24.

board of three appointed for founding citizen colonies, and also Marcus Fulvius Flaccus. Admittedly the Gracchi, in their eagerness for victory, went too far. But good men should be prepared to submit even to injustice rather than do wrong in order to defeat it. As it was, the nobles took advantage of their victory to indulge their desire for revenge: they killed or banished numbers of people – conduct which did little to increase their power, but rather caused them to live the rest of their lives in fear. This is what generally ruins great states – when each party will stick at nothing to overcome its opponents, and having done so, takes vengeance on them without mercy. However, party animosities and political morality in general are an inexhaustible subject, and the detailed discussion that its importance deserves would occupy more space than I have at my disposal. So I will resume my interrupted narrative.

CHAPTER VI

METELLUS'S FIRST CAMPAIGN (109 B.C.)

I. OCCUPATION OF VAGA; BATTLE AT THE RIVER MUTHUL

AFTER Aulus Albinus's conclusion of the treaty, and the shameful flight of the Roman army, the consuls-elect Metellus and Silanus* had arranged together about the province each should take, and Metellus had obtained Numidia. He was an energetic man, who, although an opponent of the popular party, enjoyed an unblemished reputation among all sections of the community. Directly he entered on his term of office, he devoted his whole attention to the war which he was going to conduct – since other business, he thought, could be left to his colleague. Having little confidence in the army already in Africa, he levied fresh troops, summoned auxiliary contingents from all quarters, laid in stocks of armour, weapons, horses, and every sort of war material, including an abundance of provisions – everything, in fact, that is commonly needed in operations on a big scale and of mixed character. In carrying out these measures the Senate helped him by acceding to all his demands, the 'Latin' and other Italian towns, as well as the client kings, by voluntarily sending reinforcements; and the whole country worked with the utmost enthusiasm. When everything was prepared and set in order to his satisfaction he started for Numidia. The people hoped for great things from him, because apart from his other good qualities he was a man

* If, as would appear from section 37, the elections had been postponed until after the start of the new year (109 B.C.), the consuls must have entered upon their office immediately upon election, in which case they should be referred to simply as 'consuls' rather than 'consuls-elect'. The alternative is to suppose that the events stated by Sallust in section 37 to have happened in January 109 B.C. really took place in the autumn or early winter of 110.

whom the prospect of wealth could not tempt. For it was the cupidity of our officers in Numidia that hitherto had broken our strength and increased that of our enemy.

On his arrival in Africa, he took over from Spurius Albinus, now acting consul, an indolent and unwarlike army, in no fit state to face danger or toil, readier to brag than to fight, and so undisciplined and ill behaved that it plundered its allies and allowed itself to be plundered by the enemy. Its demoralized condition caused its new commander so much anxiety that he could entertain little hope of being helped much by its numerical strength. Although the time available for the summer campaign had been shortened by the postponement of the elections and he had no doubt that his fellow citizens were awaiting its result with eager impatience, he decided not to take the field until he had inured the men to hard labour by putting them through a course of old-fashioned training. For Albinus had been so dismayed by the disaster which had befallen his brother Aulus and his army that he had determined not to move out of the Province; and for most of that part of the campaigning season during which he was in command he had kept the soldiers in permanent camps, moving them only when the bad smell or lack of fodder compelled him. The camps were not fortified, nor were watches posted in accordance with military routine; and men absented themselves from duty whenever they pleased. Camp-followers and soldiers roamed about together at all hours of day and night, plundering the fields, taking forcible possession of farmhouses, and trying which of them could carry off most cattle and slaves to barter with traders for imported wine and other commodities. They even sold their corn rations and bought what bread they needed each day. In short, every imaginable vice that one would expect to find among a set of dissipated idlers was to be found in that army – and some new ones as well.

In handling this difficult situation Metellus seems to have

shown his greatness and prudence no less than in the actual conduct of the war, steering a judicious course between popularity-seeking and undue severity. He started, it is said, by putting a stop to practices which encouraged idleness. No one, he decreed, was to sell bread or any other cooked food in camp; the camp-followers were sent about their business; both ordinary privates and front-line troops were forbidden to keep servants or beasts of burden either in camp or on the march;* and other irregular practices were strictly controlled. Furthermore, he moved camp daily, making a series of cross-country marches, and each new camp was fortified with a rampart and trench, as though the enemy were close at hand. At night he placed sentry-posts at short intervals and went the rounds himself, accompanied by his officers. On the march, too, he moved to and fro between the head and the tail of the column, often keeping for some time in the middle, to see that no one left the ranks, that the men kept close together round their standards, and that each soldier carried his food and arms. By these methods he was able to prevent breaches of discipline, and without having to inflict many punishments he soon restored the army's morale.

Jugurtha was informed by his spies of these activities, and on hearing from his friends in Rome that Metellus was incorruptible he began to feel dubious about his chances of victory and at last made a genuine attempt to arrange terms of surrender. He sent envoys to the consul in the guise of suppliants, with orders to ask only that his own and his children's lives should be spared, and to surrender everything else at discretion. But the experience of his predecessors had taught Metellus how untrustworthy and fickle the Numidians were

* No wonder they tried to obtain porters or mules: for Roman armies used a bare minimum of transport, and the soldiers were burdened not only with their armour, weapons, and personal possessions, but with rations for a fortnight or so, entrenching tools, and stakes for making palisades round their camps – a formidable load to carry under an African sun.

and how often they changed their minds. So he approached each of the envoys separately and discreetly sounded them; and when he found that they could be used to serve his turn, he induced them by lavish promises to deliver Jugurtha to him, alive if possible, but, failing that, dead. In a public audience, however, he told them to take back a favourable reply to the king. A few days later, with his army on the alert and prepared for instant battle, he marched into Numidia, where there was nothing to indicate a state of war: the cottages were full of people, and cattle and labourers were in the fields. The king's officials came out from the towns and hamlets to meet the Romans, offering to furnish corn, convey supplies, and carry out any other orders. But Metellus did not relax his precautions on that account. Just as if an enemy were close at hand, he advanced with his column carefully protected, reconnoitring to some distance in every direction, because he thought these indications of submission were a ruse designed to lead him into a trap. Accordingly, he himself marched at the head of the column with some lightly equipped cohorts and a picked force of slingers and archers; his lieutenant Gaius Marius acted as rear-guard with the cavalry.* The auxiliary cavalry was divided between the two flanks under the command of military tribunes and the prefects of the auxiliary cohorts, and skirmishers were interspersed among the ranks of this cavalry, to repel attacks made at any point by squadrons of enemy horse. For Jugurtha was so crafty, so well acquainted with the country, and so experienced in warfare, that one never knew which was the more deadly – his presence or his absence, his offers of peace or his threats of hostilities.

Not far from the route which Metellus was taking lay the Numidian town called Vaga, which was the most frequented

* i.e. Roman, or at any rate Italian, cavalry, as distinguished from the auxiliary cavalry, which consisted partly – in this passage perhaps wholly – of foreigners.

market in the whole kingdom: many Italians used to settle there for purposes of trade. The consul installed a garrison in this town in order to test the feeling of the inhabitants and – supposing they acquiesced – to obtain a good point of vantage. He also had stores of corn and other material collected there, thinking, as was reasonable in the circumstances, that the presence of so many traders would facilitate the provisioning of the army and also safeguard the stocks he had already obtained. During these operations Jugurtha redoubled his efforts to secure peace, sending envoys to make humble entreaty to Metellus and to offer to surrender everything except his life and that of his children. Metellus adopted the same tactics with these envoys as he had with their predecessors: he seduced them into betraying their master, and then sent them home, not giving the king an answer one way or the other to his request for peace terms, but playing for time until they could perform what they had promised.

When Jugurtha compared Metellus's words with his actions, he realized that his own technique was being used against him: ostensibly, peace was offered him, but in reality it was war to the knife. He had been deprived of one of his largest cities, and the enemy had made themselves familiar with his country and tampered with the loyalty of his subjects. In this state of affairs he had no choice but to fight it out. Accordingly he took careful note of his enemy's line of march; and since the terrain seemed to offer him a chance of gaining a victory, he mustered as large forces of every kind as he could, and by following out-of-the-way bypaths got ahead of Metellus's army.

In the part of Numidia that the partition had assigned to Adherbal there was a river flowing from the south called the Muthul,* and about twenty miles away from it a parallel range of hills which was naturally barren and had remained un-

* Probably the Mellègue, a tributary on the right bank of the Medjerda.

cultivated. From its middle projected a sort of spur, immensely long and clothed with wild olives, myrtles, and other trees such as will grow in a dry sandy soil. The plain lying between the hills and the Muthul was uninhabited owing to the lack of water, except the parts close to the river, which were planted with shrubs and populated by husbandmen and their livestock. On the spur which, as I said, extends at right angles from the mountain range, Jugurtha drew up his army in a thinly extended line. He put his elephants and a part of his infantry under command of Bomilcar, and gave him instructions how to act. Jugurtha took up his own position nearer the mountain with all his cavalry and the pick of the infantry. Then, visiting in turn each squadron and company, he earnestly besought them to remember the victory which their valour had already gained and to defend him and his kingdom against the greed of the Romans. 'You are about to fight,' he said, 'with men whom you have beaten before and compelled to pass under a yoke. They have a new commander, but that does not make them any braver than they were. I have given you everything that a general can be expected to provide for his troops. You have the advantage of position, and you know what you are about, while they have no notion what is in front of them. You are neither outnumbered nor outclassed. So be on the alert and ready to attack the Romans when the signal is given. This day will either end all your labours and crown your victories, or else usher in the most grievous calamities.' He also addressed individually every man whom he had rewarded with a gratuity or honour for distinguished service, reminding him of the fact and pointing him out as an example to others; and finally, adapting his mode of address to each man's character – using in turn promises, threats, and entreaties – he sought to inspire courage in the soldiers at large. Just at this moment Metellus, who was unaware of the enemy's presence, descended the mountain at the head of his army and saw them. At first he could not make out what the unusual sight meant: for the Numidians had stationed themselves and their horses among the thickets, and although they were not completely hidden by the low trees, it was difficult to distinguish just what was there, since the men and their standards were concealed both by their surroundings and by camouflage. But he soon detected the ambush and ordered a brief halt, during which he altered his formation. On his right flank, which was nearest the enemy, he posted three reserve lines; he distributed slingers and archers between the companies of infantry, stationed all his cavalry on the wings, and after a brief address – which was all that there was time for – led the army down into the plain in its new formation, with what had been its front marching at right angles to the direction of the enemy.

He noticed that the Numidians did not descend the hill but stayed still. Fearing – in view of the summer heat and the scarcity of water – that his army might succumb to thirst, he sent forward his lieutenant Rutilius* to the river, with the light-armed cohorts and a part of the cavalry, to occupy a position for a camp before Jugurtha could prevent him. For he expected that the enemy, being doubtful of success in a pitched battle, would delay his progress by frequent skirmishes and flank attacks, in the hope that fatigue and thirst would force his soldiers to acknowledge defeat. Then, taking careful note of the changing situation and the nature of the ground, he began to advance slowly in the order in which he had descended, keeping Marius where he would be ready to take command behind the front line of battle, while he himself was with the left-wing cavalry, which had now become the head of the column of route. When Jugurtha saw that Metellus's rear-

* Publius Rutilius Rufus (consul 105 B.C.), a friend of Scipio Aemilianus, with whom he served at the siege of Numantia in 133, was a *legatus* in Africa under Metellus. His condemnation in 92 on a notoriously false charge of extortion did much to bring the Equestrian juries into disrepute.

guard had passed the first lines of his own army, he stationed a force of some two thousand infantry on the hill at the point where Metellus had descended, so that if the Romans should give ground they would not be able to retreat to it and defend themselves there. Immediately afterwards he gave the signal to attack. The rear of Metellus's column suffered heavy casualties, and both flanks were harassed by mobile assailants who pressed home their attacks and spread general confusion in the Roman ranks. For even the men who resisted with the most dogged courage were disconcerted by this irregular manner of fighting, in which they were wounded at long range without being able to strike back or come to grips with their foe. Jugurtha's horsemen had been given careful instructions beforehand. Whenever a squadron of the Roman cavalry began a charge, instead of retiring in a body in one direction, they retreated independently, scattering as widely as possible. In this way they could take advantage of their numerical superiority. If they failed to check their enemy's charge, they would wait till the Romans lost their formation, and then cut them off by attacks in their rear or on their flanks; and when any of the Numidians found it more convenient to retreat to the hill than to keep to the plain, their horses, being used to the ground, made their way easily through the thickets, while ours were impeded by their inexperience of such rough country.

The whole engagement presented a changeable and indecisive aspect, such as could not but arouse feelings of horror and pity. Separated from their comrades, some retreated, while others pursued the enemy. Without any attempt to keep close to the standards or preserve formation, each man stood his ground where he found himself in danger, and tried to defend himself. Arms, missiles, horses, men – enemies and friends – were all mingled in confusion; without plan or command, everyone acted at random. Consequently, at a late hour the outcome was still in doubt. When all were faint with exertion and the heat of the day, Metellus observed that the Numidian attack was weakening. Gradually, therefore, he got his men together, re-formed the ranks, and opposed four legionary cohorts to the enemy's infantry, a large part of which had now retired to the higher ground and sat down overcome with weariness. He earnestly begged the soldiers not to lose heart, or allow a fleeing foe to be victorious, reminding them that they had no camp or fortification of any kind to retreat to, but must rely solely on their arms. Meanwhile Jugurtha on his part did not remain inactive. He went round encouraging the Numidian troops and renewed the fight, putting himself at the head of a picked body of soldiers and leaving nothing untried: he brought aid to his own men, pressed hard any of the Romans who wavered, and kept those who stood firm engaged by long-range attacks.

Such was the struggle that took place between these two great generals. In themselves they were well matched, but the resources at their disposal were very different. Metellus could rely on the courage of his soldiers, but the ground was against him. Jugurtha had everything in his favour except the quality of his troops. Eventually, the Romans realized that retreat was impossible for them, and that their enemy did not want to fight a pitched battle. So, as evening was now coming on, they stormed the hill facing them (these were the orders they had been given) and forced their way up it. The Numidians were dislodged from their position and routed. Only a few were killed: most of them were saved by their agility and by the Romans' lack of acquaintance with the country.

Bomilcar, who, as already explained, had been placed by Jugurtha in charge of the elephants and part of the infantry, had waited till Rutilius passed him, and had then led his men down gradually into the plain. While Rutilius advanced at full speed towards the river to which he had been dispatched, Bomilcar quietly adopted the battle-formation required by the situation, without ceasing to watch every movement of his enemy. He was informed that Rutilius had now encamped, suspecting no danger; but as it was also reported that the shouting from the battle in which Jugurtha was engaged was getting louder, he feared lest Rutilius should discover what was happening and go to the aid of his hard-pressed countrymen. Accordingly, he altered the formation of his battle line, which, because he distrusted his men's courage, he had drawn up in close order. He now extended it so that he would be able to block the enemy's line of march, and in this order advanced on Rutilius's camp.

The Romans suddenly noticed with surprise a great cloud of dust – being unable to see to any distance because of a plantation of trees. At first they thought it was the powdery soil being blown about by the wind; but when they saw that it did not come and go but got steadily nearer – as the enemy's line advanced – they realized what it was, and hastily snatching their arms they posted themselves in front of the camp in accordance with their orders. As soon as the enemy came close, both sides charged with loud shouts. The Numidians stood their ground only as long as they thought they could rely on their elephants for protection. When they saw the beasts getting entangled in branches of trees, with the result that they were separated and could be surrounded by the enemy, they took to their heels. Most of them, dropping their arms, escaped unhurt, thanks to the proximity of the hill and the oncoming darkness. Four elephants were taken, and all the remaining forty were killed. The Romans were glad enough to take a rest, wearied as they were with marching, fortifying their camp, and fighting. Nevertheless, as Metellus failed to appear when he was expected, they marched out to meet him, in good order and on the alert: for the cunning tactics of the Numidians forbade any carelessness or relaxation of vigilance. The night was so dark that when the two Roman armies came close together the sound of their footsteps made each of them imagine at first that an enemy was approaching, and caused much alarm and commotion – a mistake which would have had deplorable consequences, had not horsemen sent forward on both sides discovered the truth just in time. As it was, fear was suddenly replaced by joy: the men hailed one another with gladness, exchanging accounts of their experiences and boasting of their valiant deeds. Such is the way of the world: after a victory, the veriest coward is allowed to brag; defeat brings discredit even on heroes.

Metellus stayed in the same camp for four days. He had the wounded carefully tended, awarded the customary distinctions to those who had done specially good service in the battles, and at a general parade complimented and thanked the whole army. 'The tasks that lie ahead of you,' he said, 'are light: face them with the same resolution. Victory is now assured; in future you will be working to obtain booty.' In the meantime, however, he sent deserters and others who seemed suitable for the task to find out where Jugurtha was and what he was doing; whether he had only a handful of men or a considerable army, and how he was taking his defeat. In fact, the king had retired to a wooded district of great natural strength, where he was mustering an army numerically stronger than his previous one, but lacking both striking-power and staying-power – since it was composed of farm labourers and graziers, not of trained soldiers. These were the only men available: for with the exception of the cavalry of the royal bodyguard, no Numidian, after a rout, returns to his post in the king's army; every man goes off where he pleases, and this is not regarded as a shameful thing for a soldier to do, because it is the custom of the country.

CHAPTER VII

METELLUS'S FIRST CAMPAIGN (109 B.C.)
II. SIEGE OF ZAMA; REBELLION AT VAGA

JUGURTHA, then, was still full of defiance, and intended to renew the war – a war which he was in a position to conduct on whatever lines he chose and in which he had an unfair advantage, since a defeat cost him less than a victory cost the Romans. Metellus decided, therefore, to alter his strategy and avoid fighting pitched battles. Accordingly he marched into the richest part of Numidia, laid waste the countryside, and captured and burnt a number of strongholds and towns that were ill fortified or ungarrisoned, massacring the men of military age and letting his soldiers take the rest of the inhabitants and their possessions as plunder. This terrorization of the population had its effect. Numbers of hostages were surrendered to the Romans, quantities of grain and other supplies were furnished, and Metellus was allowed to install garrisons wherever he thought it necessary. These operations frightened Jugurtha much more than any defeat could have done. For the only policy which offered him any hope of success was to retreat, and now he was forced to go after the Romans; he had failed to defend an area under his own control, and now he must fight in territory occupied by the enemy. He chose what he thought was the best course open to him in the circumstances. Leaving the main body of his troops where it was, he himself followed Metellus with a picked force of cavalry, and by travelling at night and avoiding frequented routes he succeeded in surprising some Roman stragglers. Most of them, caught without arms, were killed, and others were taken prisoner; not one escaped unwounded. Before help could be sent from the camp, the Numidians, in accordance with their orders, retired to the neighbouring hills.

In Rome, meanwhile, there was great rejoicing when news came of Metellus's achievements – how he had restored old-time discipline in the army and was equally strict in his own conduct; how, though forced to fight on disadvantageous ground, he had gained a victory by his pluck; how he was making himself master of the enemy's country and had compelled Jugurtha, whom Albinus's slackness had filled with such presumption, to try to save himself by retreating into the desert. For these successes the Senate voted a public thanksgiving to the gods. The citizens who previously had been nervous and anxious about the outcome of the war were in great spirits, and Metellus's reputation stood very high.

This made him redouble his efforts for victory. While using every means to achieve it quickly, however, he took care to give his enemy no opening. He remembered that success always invites envy, and the higher his fame stood the more cautious he became. After Jugurtha's surprise attack he no longer permitted plundering by scattered parties. When grain or fodder was needed, some infantry cohorts and the whole of the cavalry stood on guard; but fire, rather than pillage, was employed as a means of devastation. Metellus led a part of the army in person and placed Marius at the head of the remainder. They encamped separately but fairly close together. Thus, when maximum striking-power was required, the whole strength of the army was available; otherwise, they spread terror and panic over a wider area by acting independently. Jugurtha meanwhile was following along a line of hills, looking for a suitable time and place to attack. Where he knew his enemy was about to pass, he would destroy the grass and contaminate the springs, which were few and far between. He used to approach near enough for Metellus or Marius to see him, skirmish with the rear of their columns, and then immediately regain the hills, threatening first one then the other, never offering battle but never letting his enemy rest – content, if he could keep them from executing their plans.

When Metellus found that his troops were being tired out by this cunning strategy, with no prospect of fighting it out, he determined to attack the large city of Zama,* the chief royal fortress of eastern Numidia. He assumed that Jugurtha would come to rescue the inhabitants from their peril because he would have no alternative, and that a battle would then ensue. But when the king heard from Roman deserters what was afoot, he got there before Metellus by making forced marches, exhorted the townspeople to defend their walls, and reinforced them with the deserters – the most reliable section of his forces, because they could not play him false. He also promised to come himself, at the right moment, with the army. After making these arrangements he withdrew to the most secluded district he could find. Shortly afterwards he learnt that Marius had been detached from the marching column, with a few cohorts, to obtain corn at Sicca, the first town to desert the king after his defeat. Jugurtha hastened there by night with the flower of his cavalry, and attacked the Romans in the gateway just as they were coming out of the town. At the same time he shouted to the townsmen to intercept them in the rear. Fortune, he said, was giving them the chance to perform a glorious exploit; if they took advantage of it, he would henceforth live in secure possession of his kingdom, and they of their liberty. And had not Marius hastened to advance against him and get clear of the town, there can be no doubt that all or most of the people of Sicca would have gone over to the enemy; for Numidians are notoriously fickle. As it was, Jugurtha succeeded in keeping his horsemen together for a time; but when the Romans assailed them with superior force and they suffered some casualties, they turned their horses' heads and made off.

* Zama Regia, in western Tunisia not far from Sicca (Le Kef).

In due course Marius rejoined Metellus before the walls of Zama. Situated in a plain, the town had little natural strength, but was equipped with fortifications and a large garrison, and well stocked with arms and other requisites. Metellus, after making such preparations as the circumstances and the nature of the ground demanded, invested the whole circuit of the walls with his army and assigned a post of command to each of his lieutenants. Then, at a given signal, loud shouts were raised simultaneously from every point of the circuit. The Numidians were undismayed and stood their ground in good order, resolute and defiant. So the struggle began. The Romans were allowed to fight as they chose. Some kept at a distance and discharged bullets or stones from slings. Others came up to the foot of the wall and tried either to undermine it or to scale it with ladders in their eagerness to get to close quarters with the enemy. The townsmen replied to these attacks by rolling down big stones on the nearest assailants and throwing pointed stakes and javelins, and also pitch mixed with sulphur and resin and ignited. Even those of our men who were too timid to go near the walls did not escape without injury, for most of them were wounded by javelins discharged from machines or by hand; thus the danger, though not the glory, was shared alike by the cowardly and the brave.

While this struggle was going on round Zama, Jugurtha raided the Roman camp at the head of a large force. The sentries were off their guard because an attack was the last thing they expected, and Jugurtha succeeded in forcing one of the gates. Disconcerted by the sudden alarm, the Roman soldiers reacted in various ways according to their characters: some tried to save themselves by flight, others seized their arms. The greater part of them were killed or wounded. Out of the whole army not more than forty men, mindful of the honour of Rome, banded themselves together and took their stand on a slight rise, from which the enemy's utmost efforts failed to dislodge them. As long as the Numidians continued to pelt them with javelins from a distance, they kept on hurling them back – and a handful of men surrounded by so many could naturally score a higher proportion of hits. If their attackers came closer, that was their opportunity to display all their valour: they hewed at them like mad until they sent them flying in disorder.

Metellus was vigorously pressing the assault on Zama, when he heard the enemy shouting behind him, and turning his horse about he saw men in full flight towards him – a sure sign that they were Romans. He instantly sent all his cavalry towards the camp, and Marius after it with some cohorts of Italians, begging him with tears, in the name of their friendship and of the Republic, not to let any reproach attach to the victorious Roman army and to see that the enemy did not escape unpunished. Marius was quick to carry out these orders. Inside the fortifications of the camp, Jugurtha found his movements hampered: some of his men were jumping down over the ramparts while others were getting in one another's way as they tried to hurry through the narrow passage-ways. So after sustaining considerable losses he retired and took cover. Metellus had still not succeeded in his attempt on the town when the approach of night compelled him to lead his army back to camp.

The next day, before going out to renew the attack, Metellus ordered all the cavalry to patrol that side of the camp on which the king would be likely to arrive, and placed military tribunes in charge of the various gates and the approaches to them. He then marched to Zama and renewed his assault on the wall. While he was absent, Jugurtha crept up stealthily and attacked the Roman horsemen. Those whose posts were nearest to the point of attack lost their nerve for the moment and were disorganized, but the rest quickly came to their aid, and the Numidians would not have been able to resist them for long, had it not been for some infantrymen whom they had interspersed among their cavalry. These did great execution in the encounter. Relying on their help, the cavalrymen, instead of adopting the usual tactics of alternate charge and retreat, rode straight forward to the attack, working their way into the Roman line and throwing it into disorder. In this way, with the help of their light-armed infantry, they nearly came off victorious.

Meanwhile a furious conflict was raging at Zama. At the points where lieutenants or tribunes were in charge, the men exerted all their strength, every man working as if success depended entirely on his own efforts. The besieged were equally active. Attacks, and preparations to meet them, were being made in every sector, and both sides were more concerned to wound their opponents than to protect themselves. Shouts of encouragement, joyful cries, and groans, rose mingled with the clash of arms to heaven, while missiles flew from side to side. But the defenders, whenever their enemy gave them a moment's respite, riveted their gaze on the progress of the cavalry engagement at the camp. As things went well or badly for Jugurtha, you could see the joy or terror in their faces; and as though their distant comrades could see and hear them, they shouted words of warning or encouragement, beckoning, gesticulating, and swaying their bodies to and fro like men hurling or avoiding missiles. When Marius noticed this – for he was in command on the side facing the camp – he purposely slackened his effort, as though he were losing confidence, and left the Numidians undisturbed to watch the action that their king and fellow countrymen were fighting. Then, when they were held spellbound by the absorbing spectacle, he suddenly made a violent onslaught on the wall. Mounting on ladders, his soldiers had almost gained the top, when the townsmen came running up and plied them with a shower of stones, firebrands, and other missiles. Our men resisted for a time; then, as one ladder after another was smashed and the men on them were hurled to the ground, the survivors got away as best they could – a few safe and sound, but the greater part severely wounded. At length night separated the combatants.

Metellus now saw that his attempt was in vain. He was no nearer to taking the town; Jugurtha would not fight except from ambush or on ground of his own choosing; and the campaigning season was over. Accordingly he raised the siege of Zama, and after placing garrisons in such of the surrendered towns as were adequately protected by their site or by fortifications, he settled the rest of the army in winter quarters in that part of the Province which adjoins Numidia. He did not, however, spend the winter months – as so many do – in idleness or dissipation. Since force had achieved so little, he now planned to use stratagem instead, by inducing the king's friends to play the traitor. Bomilcar – the man who had accompanied Jugurtha to Rome and after giving bail had fled to escape trial for the murder of Massiva – was in the best position to betray him because he was his best friend. So Metellus tempted him with many promises. He began by getting Bomilcar to meet him at a secret conference; then, by pledging his word that if he delivered up the king, alive or dead, the Senate would grant him a free pardon and allow him to keep all his property, he easily prevailed on him; for the Numidian was of a treacherous disposition, and feared that if peace were made with Rome the terms of the treaty would include his own surrender for execution.

At the first convenient opportunity he went to see Jugurtha, who was in low spirits and complaining bitterly of his ill fortune. With tears in his eyes Bomilcar urged him to take thought, before it was too late, for himself, for his children, and for the people of Numidia who had served him so well. He reminded him that they had been defeated in every battle, that his country had been ravaged, many of his subjects taken prisoner or killed, and the resources of the kingdom seriously impaired. 'You have tried your luck often enough now,' he said, 'and have made enough demands on your soldiers' courage; if you hesitate any longer, you may find that the Numidians will take the matter into their own hands.' By such arguments he induced the king to surrender. An embassy was sent to the Roman commander to say that Jugurtha was ready to comply with any orders he might give and to place himself and his kingdom unconditionally at his disposal. Metellus at once ordered all men of senatorial rank serving with the army to come from the camp, and together with such other persons as he thought fit, called them to a council of war. In conformity with traditional usage, he accepted the decision of the council and communicated it to Jugurtha's envoys. The king was to surrender two hundred thousand pounds of silver, all his elephants, and a quantity of arms and horses. These demands being promptly complied with, Metellus next commanded all the deserters to be brought to him in chains. Most of them were delivered up; a few, however, as soon as the negotiations began, had fled into Mauretania to King Bocchus. When Jugurtha, after being stripped of arms, troops, and money, was told to come to Tisidium in person to receive the consul's commands, he began once more to waver in his resolution; for his guilty conscience made him fear the punishment that he deserved. For many days he hesitated, sometimes feeling so mortified at his defeat that anything seemed better than to go on with the war, while at another moment he would reflect how grievous a fall it was for a king to become a slave. Finally – although he had already thrown away to no purpose his most effective means of defence – he determined to renew hostilities. In Rome, meanwhile, the Senate had discussed the distribution of provinces and had assigned Numidia to Metellus.*

* i.e. Metellus was to retain his command, as proconsul, for the year 108.

Shortly before this it happened that Gaius Marius was offering a sacrifice at Utica. The soothsayer who inspected the entrails of the victims declared that a great and marvellous destiny awaited him. Accordingly, if he had any projects in mind, he could undertake them with full confidence in the will of heaven; and he should seize every opportunity of pushing his fortune, since all his enterprises would prosper. Even before this, Marius had been obsessed by an ardent longing for the consulship – an office for which he had every qualification except blue blood. He was a hard worker, a man of integrity, and an experienced soldier. Indomitable on the battlefield, he was frugal in his private life, proof against the temptations of passion and riches, and covetous only of glory. His birthplace was Arpinum,* where he had spent all his boyhood. Directly he reached military age, he had gone on active service and set himself to learn the art of warfare; for he was not interested in Greek rhetoric or the elegant accomplishments of a man about town. It was a sound training for a young man: protected from demoralizing influences, his character had quickly matured. So when he first presented himself before the Assembly as a candidate, for the post of military tribune, though few people knew him by sight, his reputation was quite enough to secure his election by the unanimous choice of all the voting tribes. He followed up this success by obtaining a series of magistracies; for in each office he so conducted himself that he was judged worthy to hold a higher one. Yet in spite of the outstanding merit he had shown hitherto (at a later stage of his career, his hankering after popularity proved his downfall), he dared not aspire to the consulship. For at that time, although citizens of low birth had access to other magistracies, the consulship was still reserved by custom for noblemen, who contrived to pass it on from one to another of their number.

* A town in central Italy, some sixty miles south-east of Rome. It was the birthplace of Cicero also.

A self-made man, however distinguished he might be or however admirable his achievements, was invariably considered unworthy of that honour, almost as if he were unclean.

When Marius found that the soothsayer's prediction pointed in the same direction as his own secret ambition, he asked Metellus for leave of absence to become a candidate. Now Metellus, though richly endowed with many of the qualities that a good citizen should wish to possess, such as courage and the love of honour, had the usual failing of the aristocrat – a haughty and disdainful spirit. He was taken aback by Marius's extraordinary proposal and did not fail to express his surprise: adopting the tone of a candid friend, he sought to dissuade him from embarking on such a misguided course and entertaining ambitions above his station. 'Do not imagine', he said, 'that all aspirations are proper to all men; be content with your lot, and do not ask of the Roman people a favour which they would have every right to refuse you.' Since these and similar arguments failed to turn Marius from his purpose, Metellus at last said that as soon as the military situation made it possible he would grant his request. And later, when Marius kept on renewing his petition, he is alleged to have told him not to be in such a hurry to be off. 'It will be time enough', he added, 'for you to stand for the consulship in the same year as my son.' Now Metellus's son, who was attached to his father's personal staff in Africa, was only about twenty years old; and this repartee served merely to inflame Marius's eagerness for the honour he coveted and to make him hate Metellus.* Desire and anger are very bad counsellors: and it was by these that Marius was now actuated. There was nothing he would not do or say to make himself popular. The soldiers under his command in the winter camp were allowed

* If this story is true, Metellus was purposely being offensive – since the earliest age at which a consulship could legally be held was forty-three, and Marius was already nearly fifty.

more indulgence than before; and in discussing the war with the large community of traders at Utica he bandied about accusations and boasts. If half the army were entrusted to him, he said, in a few days he would have Jugurtha in chains; the commander-in-chief was deliberately prolonging the war because his vain and tyrannical pride made him too fond of power. These complaints impressed his hearers all the more because the long continuance of the war had ruined them, and for impatient men everything moves too slowly.

There was with the Roman army a Numidian called Gauda, a son of Mastanabal* and grandson of Masinissa; Micipsa had nominated him in his will as his heir in the second degree. This man, who was diseased and not in full possession of his faculties, had petitioned to be allowed, in virtue of his royal status, to have a seat next to that of the consul; and later he demanded also a squadron of Roman cavalry as a bodyguard. Metellus refused both requests – the seat of honour, on the ground that it was customarily granted only to persons on whom the Roman people had formally conferred the title of king; the guard, because it would be an insult for Roman horsemen to be attached as attendants to a Numidian. While Gauda was smarting under this rebuff he was approached by Marius, who offered to help him pay the general out for the affronts put upon him and egged on his feeble intellect by playing up to his conceit – telling him that he was a king, a great personage, a grandson of the famous Masinissa. 'If Jugurtha is captured or killed,' he said, 'you will immediately become the ruler of Numidia; and that may happen very soon if I am elected consul and sent to take command.' By such means he won over not only Gauda but also a number of Roman Equites who were either serving in the army or engaged in trade, persuading them, partly by his personal influence and partly by raising their hopes of peace, to write

* Jugurtha's father.

to their friends in Rome severely criticizing Metellus's conduct of the war and demanding that Marius should be given the command. In this way he secured a large body of supporters who urged his claims to the consulship in the most complimentary terms; and just at that particular time the commons, taking advantage of the defeat inflicted on the nobles by the law of Mamilius, were doing all they could to get new men elected. Thus everything favoured Marius.

Meantime Jugurtha, after deciding to reopen hostilities instead of surrendering, was taking great pains to get everything ready with the utmost dispatch. He was levying a fresh army, trying by threats or offers of reward to regain the towns which had deserted him, and fortifying places already in his possession. The armour, weapons, and other material that he had surrendered in the hope of obtaining peace, were replaced by making or buying fresh supplies, and bribes were offered not only to the Romans' slaves but even to the soldiers on garrison duty. In short there was nothing he kept his hands off, nothing that his ceaseless activity left alone. His importunity prevailed upon the inhabitants of Vaga, a town in which Metellus had placed a garrison when Jugurtha was beginning to treat for peace. The leading citizens had never wanted to desert their king, and now plotted to betray the town to him. As for the proletariat, they were as fickle as most proletariats are – especially in Numidia: always ready for a rebellion or a fight, they loved change and had no liking for peace and quiet. In due course the conspirators agreed to make their coup on the next day but one, because it was a day celebrated as a festival* throughout Africa, on which fun and frolic might be expected rather than any cause for alarm. When the time came, the centurions, military tribunes, and the commandant himself, Titus Turpilius Silanus, were invited to various houses, and all except Turpilius had their throats cut at the

* The date of this festival is recorded. It was held on 13 December 109 B.C.

dinner table. The assassins next attacked some soldiers who were strolling about unarmed – since it was a holiday and their officers were absent. The mob followed their example, some because the noblemen had told them to do so, others just because they enjoyed that kind of thing; no matter that they had no idea of what had been done or what design was afoot: some fresh excuse for a riot was all they wanted.

Disconcerted by the sudden peril and not knowing what best to do, the Roman soldiers were much alarmed. They could not reach the citadel where their standards and shields were, because the way was barred by a hostile force; flight was out of the question because the gates had been shut before the attack. Moreover women and children perched on the edges of the housetops were pelting them as hard as they could with stones and anything else they could find there. Unable to guard against dangers threatening from two directions at once, the bravest men could do nothing even against such feeble assailants: good soldiers and bad soldiers, courageous and cowardly, were cut down together with none to avenge them. In this massacre, perpetrated by a savage enemy in a completely closed city, the commandant Turpilius was the only Italian who got away unhurt. Whether he owed his escape to his host's compassion, or to a secret bargain, or simply to luck, I have not discovered. In any case, a man who in such a calamity could prefer dishonourable survival to an untarnished name must have been a detestable wretch.

The news of these events at Vaga affected Metellus to such a degree that for a short while he shut himself up in his quarters. After a time, he was moved to anger as well as grief, and bent all his thoughts on taking speedy vengeance for the outrage. He called out the legion that was with him in the winter camp and mustered as many Numidian horsemen as he could. Just as the sun set he marched them out, unencumbered by baggage, and about the third hour of the next day they reached a plain surrounded by somewhat higher ground. By this time the soldiers were tired out with their long march and in no mood for any further exertion. So Metellus told them that the town of Vaga was not more than a mile away, and that they ought to endure patiently such toil as still lay before them for the sake of avenging the unhappy fate of their brave fellow-countrymen. He also held out to them the prospect of rich booty. After rousing their spirits by these means, he ordered the cavalry to take the lead in extended order and the infantry to follow in the closest possible formation, with their standards concealed.

When the people of Vaga saw an army advancing towards them, they first conjectured rightly that it was Metellus, and closed their gates. Later, noticing that their land was not being pillaged and that the head of the column was composed of Numidian horsemen, they decided that it must be Jugurtha and went out to meet him with great rejoicing. Suddenly, at a signal, cavalry and infantry attacked: some massacred the crowd that had poured out of the town, while others rushed to the gates or seized the towers, forgetting fatigue in their rage and their hope of booty. Thus the men of Vaga had but two days' joy of their treachery: their large and wealthy town was completely destroyed to satisfy the Romans' desire for vengeance and plunder. Turpilius, who, it will be remembered, had been the only man to escape, was put on trial by Metellus, and as he could offer no satisfactory defence, he was convicted. His punishment was flogging and execution – for he possessed the rights only of a 'Latin' citizen.

Meanwhile Bomilcar, who had induced Jugurtha to start the negotiations for surrender which fear had afterwards caused him to discontinue, had become suspect in the eyes of the king, whom he himself now distrusted. He therefore sought a change of régime and cudgelled his brains day and night for some stratagem to compass Jugurtha's destruction.

Trying every possible means of effecting his purpose, he finally obtained the help of Nabdalsa, a rich and distinguished nobleman who was very popular with his compatriots. This man was frequently placed in sole command of the army during Jugurtha's absence, and was entrusted with all such business as fatigue or preoccupation with more important matters prevented the king from attending to personally – marks of confidence which had brought him fame and wealth. The two of them put their heads together and fixed a day for their treacherous attack; the details, they decided, could best be arranged on the spur of the moment, as circumstances might dictate. Nabdalsa then went to rejoin the army, which he had orders to keep on the move between the various winter encampments of the Romans, so that the country could not be ravaged without the enemy's suffering for it. The enormity of his intended crime, however, made him lose his nerve: he failed to appear at the time agreed upon, and by his pusillanimity held up the execution of the design. Bomilcar was eager to get on with it and felt anxious lest his accomplice, in his frightened state, should abandon his original intention and adopt some fresh line of action. So he sent trustworthy messengers to him with a letter, in which he upbraided his weakness and cowardice, and calling to witness the gods by whom Nabdalsa had sworn, warned him not to let the rewards Metellus had offered prove their ruin. Jugurtha's end, he argued; was near at hand; the only question was whether he should perish by their bold action or by that of Metellus. So Nabdalsa had better consider which he preferred – rewards or torture.

At the moment when this letter was delivered it chanced that Nabdalsa, tired out by exercise, was resting on his bed. Bomilcar's message threw him into a state of anxiety and distress; and after a time, as often happens in such circumstances, he was overcome by sleep. He had a Numidian secretary, a man who enjoyed his confidence and affection and was privy to all his plans, with the exception of this latest project. On hearing that a letter had come, this man assumed that his help or advice would be required as usual. So he entered the tent while his master slept, picked up the letter, which Nabdalsa had carelessly dropped on his pillow, and after reading it through went straight to the king with news of the plot he had discovered. Nabdalsa woke up shortly afterwards. When he found that the letter was missing and heard from the slaves exactly what had occurred, he first of all tried to pursue the informer. Failing in this attempt, he went to Jugurtha in the hope of pacifying him. He declared that he himself had intended to disclose the plot but had been anticipated by his disloyal retainer; and with tears he begged Jugurtha, in the name of their friendship and his previous faithful service, not to think him capable of such a crime. To these protestations the king replied with a mildness which merely served to cloak his real feelings. He summarily executed Bomilcar and a number of others whom he found to be implicated in the plot; but he then contrived to smother his anger, for fear of provoking an insurrection. From that moment, however, he knew no repose by day or night. Never did he feel safe at any place or in any man's company – for now he feared his subjects as much as the enemy. His eyes were all round him, he trembled at every sound, and slept at night in many different places, some of them ill suited to the dignity of a king. Often, starting out of his sleep, he would clutch his arms and raise an alarm – so harassed was he by a terror verging on madness.

CHAPTER VIII

METELLUS'S SECOND CAMPAIGN (108 B.C.)

WHEN Metellus heard from deserters of the discovery of the plot and the fate of Bomilcar, he made up his mind that the war must be started all over again, and hastily renewed his preparations. Marius kept on asking for leave of absence; and since Metellus did not want to have about him a man who was discontented and bore him a personal grudge, he sent him home. The Roman populace, on learning the contents of the letters that had been written concerning Metellus and Marius,* had readily believed the assertions made about them. Metellus's noble birth, which formerly had been regarded as a distinction, now made him unpopular, while his rival's humble origin won him increased favour. In both cases, however, it was party spirit, rather than their real merits or defects, that influenced people's minds. Moreover, seditious tribunes were exciting the mob: in every public meeting they demanded Metellus's head and exaggerated the virtues of Marius. In the end the lower classes were roused to such a pitch that all the artisans and peasants, whose ability to earn or to obtain credit depended solely on the labour of their hands, left their work to follow Marius about, regarding their own needs as less important than his advancement. The result was that the nobles were defeated, and for the first time in many years a newcomer to politics was elected consul. Later on, when the tribune Titus Manlius Mancinus called on a fully attended Assembly of the People to choose a commander for the Jugurthine war, they all voted for Marius. A decree which the Senate had passed shortly before, retaining Metellus in his command, was thus rendered ineffective.

* See above, section 65[4].

By this time Jugurtha had lost all his friends, most of whom he had himself put to death, while the rest in their fear had taken refuge either with the Romans or with King Bocchus. Unable to carry on the war without generals, and afraid to try the fidelity of new friends when his old ones had proved so treacherous, he kept hesitating and changing his mind. No man, no immediate measure or plan for the future, could satisfy him. He changed his officers and his marching orders from day to day, first advancing against the enemy in the hope of victory, then seeking to save himself by retreating into the desert, and he had as little confidence in the courage of his subjects as he had in their loyalty. Thus in whatever direction he turned his thoughts, everything seemed to be against him. He was still procrastinating when Metellus suddenly appeared with his army. The king prepared his men for battle and marshalled them as best he could in this emergency, and the engagement began. In the sector where he was present they resisted for some time, but all the rest of his troops were routed and chased off the field at the first charge. The Romans captured a quantity of arms and standards, but only a few prisoners; for in almost any battle the Numidians find that their legs protect them better than their weapons.

By this defeat Jugurtha was reduced to even greater despair. With the deserters and a part of his cavalry he made his way into the desert, and so to the large and rich city of Thala,* where most of his treasure was, and also a splendid establishment for the education of his children. When Metellus heard of this move, although he knew that between Thala and the nearest river there lay fifty miles of waterless desert, yet in the hope of ending the war by gaining possession of the city he determined to surmount every difficulty, even to defeat nature herself. Accordingly he issued orders that every pack animal should be relieved of all luggage, and nothing carried

* The site of this town has not been identified.

but ten days' rations of grain, together with skins and other containers for water. He also scoured the countryside to find as many tame cattle as possible and loaded them with vessels of every description – mostly wooden ones – which he obtained from the huts of the Numidians. Then he told the local inhabitants, who had surrendered to him after the king's defeat, to bring each of them as much water as he could, and fixed a time and place at which they were to deliver it. In the meantime he loaded up with water drawn from the river referred to above as being the nearest to Thala, and with this supply began his march. On reaching the place where he had arranged for the Numidians to meet him, he had only just pitched and fortified a camp when suddenly there was such a downpour of rain – so it is said – that it alone provided more than enough water for the army's needs. Furthermore, the supply brought by the Numidians proved to be larger than he expected, because, like most people who have lately submitted to a conqueror, they had exerted themselves to do more than was required of them. But the soldiers, from feelings of religious awe, preferred to use the rain water, and the incident greatly encouraged them by making them think that they were under the special care of the gods. The next day they surprised Jugurtha by arriving before the walls of Thala. The townspeople, who had supposed themselves to be protected by the difficulty of the ground, were disconcerted by the Romans' unprecedented feat, but they did not relax their preparations for the coming conflict; and our own men were equally active.

The king now believed that there was nothing Metellus could not accomplish, since his energy had overcome all obstacles – armour and weapons, terrain, seasons, even nature herself, to whom all others had to submit. So with his children and a great part of his treasure he fled from the town by night, and thereafter did not stay anywhere longer than one day or one night. He always pretended that urgent business necessitated his departure; but in fact he feared treachery, which he imagined he could avoid by rapid movement – his idea being that such designs can only be formed when there is ample time to wait for a favourable opportunity. When Metellus saw that the defenders of Thala were bent on fighting it out and that the place was protected both by its situation and by fortifications, he encircled the walls with a stockade and trench. Then, in the two best spots available, he moved forward mantlets and threw up a mound, on which towers were erected to provide cover for his siege works and for the workmen. The besieged were equally prompt with their counter-measures. Both sides strained every nerve. Eventually, after six weeks' exhausting labour and fighting, the Romans got possession of the town, but were cheated of the booty they had hoped for, because it was all destroyed by their own deserters. These men, when they saw the walls being breached by the battering-rams and realized that all was lost, carried the gold, silver, and other valuables to the royal palace. There, after gorging themselves with food and wine, they made a bonfire of the treasure and the palace and allowed the flames to consume their own bodies as well, thus inflicting upon themselves the very punishment they feared from the hands of their foes in case of defeat.

At this moment envoys came to Metellus from the town of Leptis,* begging him to send a garrison there and an officer to command it. They said that an intriguing nobleman named Hamilcar was trying to seize control of the town, and that neither the authority of the magistrates nor the laws could restrain him. Unless Metellus intervened at once, they would soon be in peril of their lives and Rome would lose a loyal ally. For at the very beginning of the Jugurthine war the people of Leptis had sent an embassy to the consul Bestia, and later to Rome itself, praying to be admitted into friendship and

* Leptis Magna (modern Lebda), in Tripolitania.

alliance. Their petition was granted, and ever since they had remained true and faithful and had used their best endeavours to execute all the orders of Bestia, Albinus, and Metellus. Therefore the latter was very willing to grant their present request. Four cohorts of Ligurians were dispatched with Gaius Annius in command.

The town of Leptis was founded by Tyrians, who are stated to have sailed there after leaving home on account of civil disturbances. It is situated between the two Syrtes, whose name is derived from their nature. They are two bays lying almost at the extreme east of Africa,* alike in character though one is larger than the other. Near the coast the water is very deep; farther out, it is a matter of chance: parts are deep, other parts, under certain weather conditions, are full of shoals. For when the sea runs high and the winds lash it into fury, the waves sweep along mud, sand, and even great rocks; thus the appearance of these bays can change completely with a shift of wind. The name *Syrtes* comes from this 'sweeping' action.† Only the language of the people of Leptis has been changed by intermarriage with Numidians. Their laws and civilization are still for the most part Tyrian. It was easier for them to retain these because of their distance from the centre of Numidian authority: for between them and the populous part of Numidia there lay extensive deserts.

The mention of this region in connexion with events at Leptis recalls to my mind a noble and memorable action of two Carthaginians, which deserves to be set on record. At the time when Carthage ruled the greater part of North Africa, Cyrene also was a large and powerful city. Between the two stretched a sandy, featureless plain, without river or mountain to

* i.e. Africa excluding Egypt, which the ancients generally regarded as part of Asia.

† Greek *σύρειν, to sweep* (almost certainly a false etymology: the name is probably indigenous).

serve as a boundary – a circumstance which involved the two peoples in a long and bitter war. On both sides armies and fleets had been defeated and put to flight, and the cities had seriously impaired each other's strength. In fear lest before long both victors and vanquished might be attacked in their exhausted state by some third party, they took advantage of a truce to make the following compact. On a specified day representatives of each city were to set out from home, and the place where they met was to be recognized as their common boundary. The Carthaginians sent two brothers called the Philaeni, who made good speed, while the Cyrenaeans travelled more leisurely. This may have been due to laziness on their part, or it might have been accidental. For in that country a storm can delay travellers just as it does at sea: the land is so flat and bare that when the wind gets up it raises clouds of sand, which are blown with great violence into their faces and eyes, so that they cannot see where they are going and must stop perforce. Now when the Cyrenaeans found themselves far outdistanced, they were afraid of being punished by their countrymen for having mismanaged the business. So they accused the Carthaginians of having started before time, and tried by various means to confuse the issue and to avoid having to admit defeat. The Carthaginians invited them to propose any other terms they liked, provided they were fair; and the Greeks gave them the choice of either being buried alive at the place where they claimed the boundary should be, or allowing them, on the same condition, to advance as far as they chose. The Philaeni accepted the proposal and gave their lives for their country. After they had been buried alive, the Carthaginians dedicated altars to the brothers on the spot, and other honours were assigned to them in the city. I shall now return to my narrative.

After the loss of Thala, Jugurtha decided that it was impossible to resist Metellus with the resources available to him. So with a small party he journeyed through the huge deserts until he reached the country of the Gaetulians, a savage, uncivilized race who at that time had never heard of Rome. Collecting a vast number of them, he trained them by slow degrees to keep ranks, follow the standards, and obey commands, and to perform the other duties of soldiers. He then approached intimate friends of King Bocchus of Mauretania, enlisting their support by lavish presents and still more lavish promises. With their aid he obtained access to the king himself, and persuaded him to take up arms against the Romans. This proved an easier and simpler matter than it might otherwise have been because at the start of the Jugurthine war Bocchus had sent envoys to Rome asking for a treaty of alliance, and his proposal – in spite of the advantage it offered for the conduct of the war just commenced – had been rejected, thanks to the intrigues of a few men who, blinded by avarice, expected to be paid for everything they did, honourable or dishonourable. Moreover, Jugurtha had married Bocchus's daughter – though it is true such a tie does not count for much with Numidians and Moors, each of whom has as many wives as he can afford; ten or more are quite usual, and kings have a proportionately larger number. Thus their affection, instead of being concentrated on a single consort, is distributed among a whole harem of women, all of them alike slightly regarded.

The two kings now assembled their armies at a place agreed upon. After they had exchanged oaths of loyalty Jugurtha tried to fire Bocchus's courage by a harangue. The Romans, he said, were men with no sense of justice and of insatiable greed, the common enemies of all mankind. They had the same motive for a war against Bocchus as they had for fighting Jugurtha himself and so many other nations – namely, their lust for empire, which made them regard all kings as potential foes. 'At the moment,' he went on, 'I am the object of their attack, as the Carthaginians were some time ago, and also King Perseus of Macedon. So it will go on: they will always choose the richest victim they can find.' After more discourse to the same effect the kings determined to march on Cirta, because in that city Metellus had placed his booty, prisoners, and baggage.* Jugurtha thought that if they could capture the place it would be a prize worth having, while if Metellus came to the rescue of the garrison they would have an opportunity of fighting him. The crafty Numidian's one concern was to involve Bocchus in hostilities as quickly as possible; for if he was allowed to procrastinate he might change his mind and give up the idea of war.

When the Roman general heard of the alliance concluded by the two kings, he was careful not to act rashly or to offer battle wherever he met the enemy, as had become his habit after defeating Jugurtha so often. He fortified a camp not far from Cirta and waited for them there, thinking that his best plan would be to see what sort of fighters his new opponents were and then to join battle when it suited him. Before taking further action he received a letter from Rome telling him that the province of Numidia had been assigned to Marius, of whose election to a consulship he had already been informed. He was more upset by the news than was right or becoming. He could neither refrain from tears nor control his tongue; for in spite of all his eminent qualities he was not manly enough to endure mortification. Some attributed his attitude to pride, others, to the indignation of a noble nature exasperated by humiliation; the common opinion was that he was provoked by seeing the victory he had all but won snatched from his hands. For my part, I am sure it was more

* It was Jugurtha's capture of Cirta (modern Constantine) that had started the war (section 26). It is strange that Sallust does not tell us how the Romans retook this natural stronghold. The explanation of his silence may be that its fortifications were destroyed at the time of the siege and never restored, in which case Metellus may have merely taken possession of a more or less unoccupied site.

Marius's advancement than his own wrongs that tormented him: he would have felt less resentment if the province taken from him had been given to anyone other than Marius.

This disappointment inhibited him from action. He thought it folly to expose himself to danger by troubling about what no longer concerned him. So he contented himself with sending a delegation to Bocchus to warn him against becoming an enemy of Rome without due cause. 'You have now a splendid opportunity', he said, 'of concluding a friendly alliance, which will be preferable to war. In spite of your confidence in your strength you should not throw away a certainty for an uncertainty. It is always easy to begin fighting, but the man who starts may find it exceedingly hard to stop; for while anyone – even a coward – can open hostilities, only the victor can decide when they shall cease. Think therefore of your safety and that of your kingdom, and do not imperil your good fortune by involving it with the hopeless prospects of Jugurtha.' The king replied to these representations in a quite conciliatory tone. He desired peace, he said, but pitied the misfortunes of Jugurtha; if the same offer were made to him also, agreement could be reached on all points. Metellus sent again to make counter-proposals, of which Bocchus accepted some and rejected others. In this way, with messages continually going to and fro, time passed and – as Metellus intended – the war remained at a standstill.

CHAPTER IX

THE NEW CONSUL (107 B.C.)

MARIUS, as I have said, had been elected consul with the enthusiastic support of the common people. When the Assembly voted the province of Numidia to him, the hostility which he had already shown towards the nobles redoubled in violence, since he thought now that he could defy them. Sometimes he denounced individuals, sometimes the whole body of the nobility, saying that his consulship was a prize which he had won by beating them, and making other remarks calculated to glorify himself and wound them. At the same time he gave first priority to preparations for the war. He demanded that the legions should be made up to strength, called for auxiliary troops from subject peoples and kings and from Rome's Italian allies, summoned the bravest soldiers from the Latin towns – men who had either served under him or been recommended to him – and by personal appeals induced time-expired veterans to join his expeditionary force. The Senate, in spite of its hostility, dared not refuse anything he asked. As to the addition to the strength of the legions, they were only too pleased to authorize it, because the people were supposed to dislike military service, so that Marius would either have to go without the men he needed or forfeit his popularity with the multitude. But they were disappointed: most of the men were eager to go overseas with Marius, imagining that they would make a fortune out of the spoils, return home victorious, and so forth. A speech which Marius made greatly increased their enthusiasm. For when he had obtained from the Senate all the decrees he demanded and the time had come to enrol the soldiers, he called a public meeting with the object both of encouraging recruitment and of making one more attack on the nobles. His address was to the following effect:

'I know, fellow citizens, how election to a post of authority seems to change most men's characters. As candidates, they are full of energy, humbly entreat your support, and behave with moderation. Once elected, they become arrogant and slothful. To my mind this is altogether wrong. Inasmuch as the whole state is more important than a consulship or praetorship, more pains should be taken over its administration than in canvassing for these offices. I am well aware of the heavy responsibility which this great honour lays upon me. To prepare for war without exhausting the public treasury, to press into military service men whom you are anxious not to offend, to direct everything at home and abroad, and to do all this in the midst of jealousy, obstruction, and intrigue, is a harder task than people imagine. Furthermore my political opponents, if they make a mistake, can rely for protection on their ancient lineage, the resources of their relatives and marriage connexions, and their numerous dependants. My hopes rest only on myself, and I must sustain them by courage and uprightness; for I have nothing else to trust in. I know, too, that everyone's eyes are upon me – that fair-minded and patriotic men wish me well because my efforts are serviceable to our country, while the nobles seek occasion to pounce on me. Wherefore I must strive all the harder to frustrate their plans and prevent your being deceived. From my childhood to this day I have so lived that every kind of toil and danger has been familiar to me; and what I did for nothing, before you conferred these honours on me, I shall not cease to do now that I have received my reward. Restraint in the use of authority is not to be expected from men who have merely assumed a mask of virtue in order to procure advancement. But I, having spent all my life in honourable pursuits, have so habituated myself to well-doing that it has become second nature to me.

'You have chosen me to conduct the war against Jugurtha, and this has greatly annoyed the nobility. Now consider whether it would be better to alter your decision – I mean, to appoint for this or for any similar work some member of that coterie of noblemen, a man with a long pedigree and a houseful of family portraits, but without a single campaign to his credit, who, faced with a serious task which he does not know the first thing about, will get excited and run about trying to find some commoner to instruct him in his duty. This is in fact what generally happens: the man you appoint to take command looks for another to command him. I myself know cases in which a consul, after his election, has taken to studying history and Greek military treatises. This is reversing the natural order of things. For although you cannot discharge the duties of an office until you have been elected to it, the necessary practical experience should come first. Compare me, the "new" man, with these high and mighty ones. What they know only from hearsay or reading, I have seen with my own eyes or done with my own hands. What they have learned out of books, I have learned on the battlefield. It is for you to judge whether words or deeds are more to the point. They scorn my lack of illustrious ancestors, I scorn their indolent habits. The worst that can be said of me is that I am a man of humble condition; *they* can be charged with acts of infamy. For my part, I believe that all men are partakers of one and the same nature, and that manly virtue is the only true nobility. If the fathers of Albinus and Bestia could be asked whether they would rather have had me or them for sons, what other answer do you think they would give than that they desired to have the best possible children? If these men think they have a right to look down on me, they ought equally to look down on their own ancestors, who, like me, had no nobility but what they earned by their merits. They are jealous of my preferment; but they have no wish to share the life of austerity and toil – yes, and of danger too – by which I have obtained it. Eaten up with pride, they live as if they scorned the honours you can bestow, and then demand them of you with the air of men who have lived honourably. They are making a grave mistake if they think that they can have it both ways – that they can enjoy, both together, things so incompatible as the pleasures of idleness and the rewards of honourable exertion. When they address you or the Senate they spend most of the time in praising their ancestors, because they fondly imagine that by dwelling on their brave exploits they enhance their own glory. On the contrary, the more illustrious the lives of their forefathers, the more shameful is their own indolence. The truth is that ancestral glory is like a torch that sheds a revealing light both on a man's virtues and on his faults. I admit, citizens, that I have nothing of this kind; but I have something much more glorious – deeds of my own that I can mention. See how unfair they are. The privilege they claim on the strength of other people's merits, they will not allow me in right of my own merits, just because I have no family portraits to show and am a newcomer to the nobility of office. Yet surely it is better to have ennobled oneself than to have disgraced a nobility that one has inherited.

'I do not need to be told that my opponents, if they choose to reply to what I have said, are quite capable of making eloquent and elaborate speeches on the subject. But since they are seizing the occasion of this high honour that you have done me to heap abuse on both of us, I have chosen to speak, in case my reticence should be interpreted as a consciousness of my unworthiness. For myself indeed – and I say this in all sincerity – no speeches can do me harm: for if they speak the truth they cannot help speaking well of me, and falsehood my life and character will refute. But since they also impugn your judgement in assigning me such a high office and so important a task, I advise you to consider again and yet again whether you will have cause to regret your choice. I cannot, to justify your confidence in me, point to the portraits, triumphs, or consulships of my ancestors. But if need be I can show spears, a banner, medals, and other military honours, to say nothing of the scars on my body – all of them in front. These are my family portraits, these my title of nobility, one not bequeathed to me, as theirs were to them, but won at the cost of countless toils and perils.

'My words are not carefully chosen. I attach no importance to such artifices, of which true merit stands in no need, since it is plainly visible to all. It is my adversaries who require oratorical skill to help them cover up their turpitude. Nor have I studied Greek literature; I had no interest in a branch of learning which did nothing to improve the characters of its professors. The lessons I have learnt are such as best enable me to serve my country – to strike down an enemy, to mount guard, to fear nothing but disgrace, to endure winter's cold and summer's heat with equal patience, to sleep on the bare ground, and to work hard on an empty stomach. These are the lessons I shall teach my soldiers. And I shall not make them go short while enjoying the best of everything myself, nor steal all the glory and leave them the toil. This is the proper way for a citizen to lead his fellow citizens. To live in luxury oneself while subjecting one's army to rigorous discipline is to act like a tyrant instead of a commander. It was by conduct such as I recommend that your ancestors won renown for themselves and for the state. Relying on that renown to shed a reflected glory on them, these noblemen, who are so different in character from those ancestors, despise us who emulate their virtues, and expect to receive all posts of honour at your hands, not because they deserve them, but as if they had a peculiar right to them. These proud men make a very big mistake. Their ancestors left them all they could – riches, portrait busts, and their own glorious memory. Virtue, they have not bequeathed to them, nor could they; for it is the only thing that no man can give to another or receive from another. They call me vulgar and unpolished, because I do not know how to put on an elegant dinner and do not have actors at my table or keep a cook who has cost me more than my farm overseer. All this, my fellow citizens, I am proud to admit. For I was taught by my father and other men of blameless life that while elegant graces befit a woman, a man's duty is to labour; that every good man should live for honour rather than for riches; that the weapons he carries in his hands, and not the furniture he keeps in his house, are the ornaments most worth having. Well then, let them continue to do what pleases them – the love-making and drinking that they set such store by; let them spend their old age as they spent their youth, in the pleasures of the table, the slaves of gluttony and lust. Let them leave the sweat, the dust, and the rest of it to us, to whom such things are better than a feast. But no: after covering themselves with infamy these rakes contrive to steal the rewards that are the due of honest men. Thus, in defiance of all justice, these foul vices of luxury and sloth are no hindrance to them in their careers; it is the innocent state that suffers ruin.

'Having said enough on that subject to defend my own character – though much less than their crimes deserve – I shall speak briefly of public affairs. In the first place, citizens, Numidia need cause you no anxiety. Hitherto Jugurtha has been saved from defeat by the greed, incompetence, or vanity of your generals; but you have now changed all this. Moreover you have an army there which knows the terrain, though its success has not been equal to its valiant efforts; for it has been gravely weakened by the corruption or rashness of its leaders. I therefore call upon all men of military age to co-operate with me in the service of our country. And no one need fear a repetition of the misfortunes which your comrades suffered under my arrogant predecessors. I shall be with you on the march and on the field of battle, to be your guide and to share your perils; and I shall claim no special privileges for myself. Rest assured that, with the gods' help, all the fruits of battle are ready to be plucked; victory, spoils, and glory await you – though even if these rewards were doubtful or remote, it would still be the duty of all patriots to rally to the aid of their fatherland. Cowardice will not enable a man to live for ever, and no parent ever prayed that his children might have immortality, but rather that they might live virtuous and honourable lives. There is more that I might say, if faint-hearts could have courage put into them by words; for the brave, I think I have said quite enough.'

Satisfied that his speech had aroused the enthusiasm of the people, Marius hastened to load his ships with stores, money, arms, and other requisites, and ordered his lieutenant Aulus Manlius to set out with the convoy. Meanwhile he continued to sign on soldiers, not, in accordance with traditional custom, from the propertied classes, but accepting any man who volunteered – members of the proletariat for the most part. Some said he did this because he could not get enough of a better kind; others, that he wanted to curry favour with men of low condition, since he owed to them his fame and advancement. And indeed, if a man is ambitious for power, he can have no better supporters than the poor: they are not concerned about their own possessions, since they have none, and whatever will put something into their pockets is right and proper in their eyes. The result of this new method of enlistment was that Marius set sail with a force considerably larger than that authorized by the decree, and a few days later he put in to Utica, where the army already in Africa was handed over to him by the lieutenant Publius Rutilius; for Metellus had avoided meeting Marius, not wishing to see what he could not bear even to hear about.

CHAPTER X

MARIUS'S FIRST CAMPAIGN (107 B.C.)

AFTER making up his legions and auxiliary cohorts to their full strength the consul advanced into a fertile region where there was abundance of spoil, all of which he let the soldiers have. He then attacked some fortresses and settlements that were badly situated for defence and ill-manned, and fought a number of small engagements in various places. In course of time the new recruits learnt to go fearlessly into action; for they saw that runaways were captured or killed, while the bravest stood the best chance of coming through unscathed, and they soon realized that the arms they carried afforded the only means of protecting liberty, fatherland, parents, and everything else, or of winning glory and riches. Thus in a short time novices and veterans were welded into a homogeneous body, all of them equally courageous. As for the two African kings, directly they heard of Marius's arrival, they separated and retired into difficult country – a plan devised by Jugurtha in the hope that before long the Romans, by dividing their forces, would expose themselves to attack; for most armies are tempted by the removal of immediate danger to relax their standards of care and discipline. Metellus meanwhile went to Rome, where, to his surprise, he was welcomed with great joy. The feeling against him had died down, and he was now as popular with the people as with the senators.

Marius acted with energy and foresight, keeping watch on his own men and on the enemy and noting their strong and weak points, observing the kings' movements, forestalling their designs and stratagems, allowing his own army no relaxation and theirs no respite from alarm. He had, for example, inflicted several defeats on the Gaetulians and on Jugurtha while they were driving off cattle seized from the inhabitants of the Province, and not far from Cirta he forced the king's own troops to abandon their arms and flee. But when he saw that these successes merely won him credit without bringing the end of the war any nearer, he decided to invest each of the towns which, by reason of their natural strength or the number of their inhabitants, were best able to help the enemy and to hinder him. This, he thought, would either deprive Jugurtha of his power of defence, if he did not interfere, or would compel him to give battle. As to Bocchus, he had several times sent word to Marius that he desired the friendship of Rome and had no intention of fighting. This may have been a ruse to enable him, by means of a surprise attack, to strike with more effect; or it may be that his natural inability to make up his mind made him thus chop and change about. The consul, in accordance with his plan, marched on various fortified towns and strongholds; some were taken by storm, others surrendered because the garrisons took fright or were seduced by Marius's bribes. At first he contented himself with minor operations, expecting that Jugurtha would fight to protect his subjects. But when he heard that the king was far away and absorbed in other tasks, he judged that the time was ripe for bigger and harder undertakings. In the middle of a huge desert lay the important and strongly defended town of Capsa,* the traditional founder of which was the Libyan Hercules. Under Jugurtha's rule its inhabitants were exempted from taxation and well treated. They were therefore particularly loyal to him, and the place was protected not only by its ramparts and a well-armed garrison, but still more by the difficulty of the surrounding country. For, except the immediate neighbourhood of the town, the whole district is desolate, uncultivated,

* The modern Gafsa, about 130 miles south of the river Muthul, at the south-eastern extremity of Jugurtha's kingdom.

waterless, and infested by deadly serpents, which like all wild animals are made fiercer by scarcity of food, and especially by thirst, which exasperates their natural malignity. Marius's mind was set on capturing this place, not only on account of its strategic importance, but also because he wanted to try his hand at what looked like a difficult enterprise, and because Metellus had won great renown by his capture of Thala, the situation and defences of which were similar, except that at Thala there were several springs of water near the walls, whereas the people of Capsa had only one never-failing supply – situated inside the town – apart from which they relied on rain water. This scarcity of water, both here and in all the comparatively uncivilized interior of North Africa, was rendered more endurable by the Numidian habit of living chiefly on milk and the flesh of wild animals and not using salt or other appetizers: they ate and drank to satisfy their hunger and thirst, not to indulge gluttonous cravings.

After making a thorough reconnaissance Marius decided – one must presume – to put his trust in heaven. For the difficulties that faced him were too formidable for human wisdom to provide against them unaided. He was even threatened by a dearth of corn, because the Numidians pay more attention to grazing than to raising crops; moreover, such grain as there was had by the king's order been conveyed into the fortresses, and the fields were parched and bare at the end of the summer. Nevertheless, Marius made such provision as his means allowed and his foresight suggested. The auxiliary horsemen were told to drive forward with the marching column all the cattle taken during the previous days. The lieutenant Aulus Manlius was sent with the light infantry to the town of Lares,* where the wage-money and reserve supplies were stored; and Marius gave out that he would come there himself

* About eleven miles south of Sicca (Le Kef).

in a few days in the course of a plundering expedition. This was said in order to conceal his real objective. He then advanced to the river Tanais.

Every day during this march he had distributed a ration of cattle to the men of each century and squadron, who were told to make water-containers out of the hides. In this way he made up for the short supply of corn and at the same time, without letting anyone discover his purpose, provided the utensils that he knew would shortly be required. By the time they reached the river, on the sixth day, they had a large stock of skins. There, after making a lightly fortified camp, he ordered the men to eat their dinners and be ready to march at sunset, abandoning their packs and taking nothing but the filled skins – as many as they themselves and their beasts could carry. In due course he set out, marched all night, and then halted. The same procedure was followed the next night; and during the third night, some time before dawn, he reached a hilly district not more than two miles from Capsa, where, with the whole army carefully screened from observation, he waited. At daybreak the Numidians, who had no reason to fear an attack, came out of the town in force, and Marius ordered all his cavalry and the swiftest of his infantry to run and occupy the gates. He was so eager for success that he hurried after them himself, to prevent the men from going after plunder. When the townspeople saw themselves thus taken by surprise, with a part of their number outside the walls and in the enemy's power, they were seized with such panic and dismay that they surrendered. Nevertheless, the town was set on fire, the adult men massacred, the remainder of the population sold into slavery, and the booty divided among the soldiers. This violation of the usages of war was not inspired by avarice or brutality on the consul's part: the fact was that the place was important to Jugurtha and difficult for the Romans to reach, and the inhabitants were a fickle and untrustworthy lot, whom neither kindness nor fear had ever been able to control.

The achievement of this noteworthy victory without any casualties enhanced still more Marius's already great reputation. Any ill-considered action on his part was now regarded as a proof of his gallantry; the soldiers, treated with consideration and enriched with plunder, praised him to the skies, while the Numidians seemed to think he had superhuman powers, so terrified were they of him; in fact everyone, friend and foe alike, believed that he either possessed divine insight or was the recipient of signs vouchsafed him by favour of the gods. After this first success he marched to other towns, and took by storm the few which resisted; the majority however had been abandoned in consequence of the terror inspired by the dreadful fate of Capsa; these he burnt, and filled all the land with bloodshed and lamentation. After capturing many places* – most of them without shedding a drop of his soldiers' blood – he embarked on a fresh enterprise, which, without being as perilous as the assault on Capsa, was equally difficult.

* These operations probably occupied a considerable time, i.e. the remainder of the year 107 and the early part of 106. Sallust says nothing about a cessation of hostilities during the winter, and in fact there may have been no cessation.

CHAPTER XI

MARIUS'S SECOND CAMPAIGN (106 B.C.)

NOT far from the river Muluccha,* which was the boundary between the territories of Jugurtha and Bocchus, was an isolated rocky hill, large enough to hold a small fort; it was exceedingly high and was accessible only by one narrow path, the other sides being as sheer as if they had been deliberately cut to make them so. As this place contained the king's treasure-house, Marius determined to put forth all his strength to capture it. Chance, however, rather than contrivance, enabled him to do so. For the fort had a large and well-armed garrison, plenty of provisions, and a spring of water; the ground was unsuitable for embankments, towers, and other siege apparatus; and the path leading to the fort was extremely narrow, with precipices on both sides. Mantlets were brought up with great danger and without result: for as soon as they had been advanced a short distance they were destroyed by fire or by stones. The slope was so steep that the soldiers could not get a footing higher up, or even move about under cover of the mantlets without risk; all the best men were being killed or wounded, and the rest were getting more and more frightened.

After spending much time and labour on the attempt, Marius became worried and began to consider whether to give it up, since all his efforts appeared fruitless, or to persevere in the hope that fortune would once again turn in his favour. For many days and nights he had been pondering the matter, unable to make up his mind, when it happened that a Ligurian, a private in an auxiliary cohort, who had left the camp to get

* Now the Moulouya, which forms the western boundary of Algeria – over 650 miles, as the crow flies, from Gafsa. It was indeed venturesome for Marius to march so far west, especially as (according to Sallust) his main body of cavalry had not yet arrived.

water and wandered to the side of the hill farthest from the fighting, noticed some snails crawling among the rocks He picked up one or two, then climbed up looking for more; and in his eagerness to collect as many as he could he gradually made his way nearly to the top. There, as he found himself quite alone, the natural human inclination to attempt something difficult turned his thoughts in a new direction. Just where he was, a big ilex happened to have grown up among the rocks; its trunk ran horizontally for a short way, then turned and rose up vertically, following the natural habit of all plants. Helping himself up either by its branches or by projecting rocks, the Ligurian managed to reach the rocky platform on which the fortress stood – since all the Numidians were intent on the battle. After carefully noting everything that he thought it would be useful later on to know, he retraced his steps, not haphazard as he had climbed up, but examining and testing every inch of the route. Then he went straight to Marius, gave him a full account of what he had done, and urged him to attack the fortress on the side where he had ascended, offering to act as a guide and to lead the way in this risky enterprise. Marius sent some of his officers with the man to explore the practicability of what he undertook to do. Their reports varied with their temperaments: some said that it was quite easy, others that it was very difficult. In spite of this difference of opinion, Marius now became somewhat more hopeful. Accordingly, choosing five of the most agile men he could find among his trumpeters and hornblowers, and four centurions, with a party of soldiers, to protect them, he ordered them all to do as they were told by the Ligurian, and fixed the following day for the operation.

After completing his arrangements and waiting for the time prescribed in his orders, the Ligurian set out. He had instructed the climbing party to change their arms and equipment. They went without helmets or shoes, so as to see better and clamber over the rocks more easily; on their backs they carried swords and shields – the latter being leather shields of Numidian pattern, which were lighter and made less noise when struck. The Ligurian led the way, fastening ropes to rocks and projecting roots of old trees to facilitate the soldiers' ascent. When some of them became nervous because they were unused to rock-climbing, he would lend them a helping hand. Where the ground was particularly difficult he sent them forward one at a time without their arms, which he carried up himself afterwards. At points where the ascent looked dangerous he insisted on trying it first himself, and encouraged his companions by going up and down several times the same way and then quickly stepping aside. At last, after a long and exhausting climb, they reached the fort, which was deserted on that side because all the defenders were, as usual, facing the enemy in front.

Marius had kept the Numidians fully engaged all day. On receiving news of the Ligurian's success he made a special appeal to his men, advancing in person beyond the mantlets and sending an assault party forward under a 'tortoise',* while large catapults, archers, and slingers harassed the enemy from a distance. The Numidians, who so often before had overturned or burnt the mantlets, were no longer in the habit of sheltering behind their ramparts: day and night they stood forward on the wall, insulting the Romans, calling Marius a madman, and threatening the soldiers with slavery at the hands of Jugurtha – for success had emboldened them. Now, while both sides were intent upon the furious struggle, the Romans fighting for glory and empire, the Numidians for their lives, trumpets suddenly rang out from behind the fort. The women and children who had come out as spectators were the first to flee; they were followed by those nearest to

* i.e. with their shields held over their heads in such a way that they overlapped and formed a protective roof.

the wall, and then by the whole of the occupants, armed and unarmed alike. At this, the Romans pressed forward all the harder and scattered their opponents, most of whom, at first, they could only wound. But before long they were making their way over corpses – racing towards the wall in their thirst for glory, and not a single man stopping to pick up booty. Thus fortune made amends for Marius's rashness, and an act for which he deserved blame won him renown.

In the meantime the quaestor Sulla had arrived at the Roman camp with a large force of cavalry, which he had been left behind to raise from the Latin and other Italian communities. Since my subject now brings this remarkable man to our notice, it seems appropriate to speak briefly of his character and manner of life; for I do not intend to write elsewhere of his career, and Lucius Sisenna,* although he has written the best and most accurate account of it, does not seem to me to have spoken with sufficient frankness. Sulla, then, belonged to a noble patrician family, but to a branch of it that had fallen into almost total oblivion because for some generations its members were lacking in energy. He had a knowledge of Greek and Latin literature equal to that of the best scholars, and was a man of large ambitions, devoted to pleasure but even more devoted to glory. His leisure hours were spent in the pursuit of enjoyment, but he never allowed it to interfere with his duties – except indeed that his behaviour towards his wife might have been more honourable. He was eloquent, shrewd, and an accommodating friend. His skill in pretence was such that no one could penetrate the depths of his mind; but he was a generous giver, especially of money. His unparalleled good fortune – up to his triumph in the civil war – was well matched by his energy, and many people have wondered

* Lucius Cornelius Sisenna (praetor 78 B.C.) was a politician and author, who wrote a history of the Social war and the Sullan civil war. He died in 67 while serving as one of Pompey's legates in the Aegean Sea.

whether he owed his success more to boldness or to luck. Of his subsequent conduct I could not speak without feelings of shame and disgust.

When Sulla, as I have said, reached Africa and presented himself at Marius's camp with his cavalry, he had no knowledge or experience of war. Yet in a short space of time he became the most skilful soldier in the army. He spoke in a friendly manner to the men and granted favours to many of them, sometimes without even waiting to be asked. Unwilling to accept favours himself if he could avoid it, he repaid those he did accept more promptly than any loan; for himself, he expected no return from those whom he benefited, but rather sought to have as many as possible indebted to him. He could converse on subjects both grave and gay with the humblest, spent much time with the men at their work, on the march, and on guard duty, and all the time refrained from the crooked conduct of seekers after popularity – for he never blackened the reputation of the consul or of any honest man. His sole concern was that no one should be his superior, and very few his equals, in counsel or in action. Such a character and such behaviour quickly endeared him to Marius and to the troops.

Now that Jugurtha had lost Capsa and other fortified towns on which he had based his defence plans, as well as a large sum of money,* he sent a message to Bocchus urging him to lead his forces into Numidia with all speed; for a pitched battle, he said, must now be fought. When he heard that Bocchus was in two minds about complying with this request, because he could not decide whether it would pay him better to participate in the war or to make peace, Jugurtha repeated his previous manoeuvre: he bribed the king's courtiers with presents and promised the Moor himself a third part of Numidia

* This treasure had been stored in the fortress on the river Muluccha, and was evidently captured with it. Its loss made it impossible for Jugurtha to continue paying his Gaetulian troops, and forced him to seek the aid of Bocchus.

if they could either expel the Romans from Africa or obtain a treaty of peace which left his own territories intact. This offer enticed Bocchus to join Jugurtha at the head of a large army. With their united forces the two kings intercepted Marius just as he was setting out for his winter encampment, and attacked him an hour or so before sunset; for they thought that the near approach of night would safeguard them if they were beaten, and – in view of their familiarity with the country – would be no hindrance to them if they won; whereas the Romans, in either event, would be hampered by the darkness. Marius had only just received reports of the enemy's approach when they were upon him. Before the army could be formed up in battle order or its baggage piled – in fact before any signal or command could be given – it was attacked by the Moorish and Gaetulian cavalry, not in line of battle or according to any regular plan, but in haphazard groups. In spite of this alarming surprise, all our men behaved with their usual courage. Some seized their arms while their comrades held the enemy at bay; some mounted their horses and made a charge. The action was more like a fight with bandits than a proper battle. Without standards or formation, horse and foot were mingled together. While some gave ground, others were cut down; and many who were desperately resisting the enemy in front found themselves surrounded from behind. Neither valour nor arms could protect them against a foe numerically superior and able to attack from every side. At length, any who happened to be standing near one another, both veterans and recruits, formed circles – which, by giving them protection and presenting an orderly front in every direction, enabled them to withstand the enemy's furious onslaught.

This dangerous situation did not frighten Marius or make him lose heart. With his bodyguard of cavalry, composed, in his case, not of personal friends but of especially brave soldiers, he scoured the whole battlefield, now bringing aid to those in difficulties, now charging the densest mass of the enemy. For it was only by joining in the fight himself that he could do anything to help his men: to issue orders amid such confusion was an impossibility. Day was now ended, but the natives showed no sign of relaxing their efforts; the kings had persuaded them that the coming of night would make things easier for them, and they continued their attacks with even greater vigour. Marius now adopted the best plan he could in the circumstances. To secure a retreat for his men, he occupied two hills close to each other. One was too small for a camp but possessed a copious spring; the other was a convenient site, because most of it was lofty and steep and needed but little fortification. Ordering Sulla and his cavalrymen to mount guard for the night near the spring, he himself gradually collected together his scattered troops – a task which was facilitated by the fact that their opponents were in equal disorder – and then withdrew them all at a rapid pace to the second hill. The strength of his position deterred the enemy from attacking it; they did not, however, let their men go far away, but surrounded both hills in force. Their soldiers then bivouacked wherever they chanced to be. Lighting a large number of fires, they spent most of the night in evincing their joy, after the manner of barbarians, by shouts and capers; even their leaders were cock-a-hoop, and – because they had not run away – strutted about like conquerors. All this was clearly visible to the Romans from the darkness of their hill-top, and it greatly encouraged them.

Marius was much reassured by seeing the enemy thus betray their lack of training. He ordered his men to maintain the strictest silence, and not even to sound the customary bugle-calls at the end of each watch. He waited till shortly before daylight, when the enemy, tired out at last, had been overcome by sleep, and then suddenly gave orders to the sentinels and to the trumpeters of the auxiliary cohorts, cavalry squadrons, and legions to sound a battle-call simultaneously, and to the soldiers to raise their war-cry and rush out of the gateways. The Moors and Gaetulians, surprised out of their sleep by this unfamiliar and terrifying noise, were incapable either of fleeing or of arming themselves – indeed, of taking any action or forming any plan. Their enemy was upon them, and no help was at hand. The shouting and din, the tumult and terror, had made them well-nigh frantic with fear. In the end they were completely routed. Most of their arms and standards were taken, and more were killed than in any previous battle; for they were too sleepy and too much dazed by the surprise to make good their escape.

Marius then resumed his march towards his winter quarters; for he had decided to winter in the coastal towns, where supplies would be obtainable. His victory did not make him careless or arrogant. Exactly as if he were in sight of the enemy, he marched in a square formation. Sulla and his cavalry were on the right, Aulus Manlius on the left with the slingers and archers, reinforced by the Ligurian cohorts. The front and rear were covered by companies of lightly equipped infantry under the command of military tribunes, and the enemy's line of march was spied out by native deserters, who knew the country best – and could best be spared if they were caught by the Numidians. At the same time the consul saw to everything in person, as though he had no subordinates in charge, going round to every section of the army and distributing praise and reprimands as they were deserved. Always fully armed and on the alert himself, he compelled the soldiers to follow his example. The precautions taken on the march were observed also in the fortification of each camp. Legionary cohorts were detailed to keep watch at the gates, auxiliary cavalry to patrol outside, and others to mount guard on top of the rampart. Marius went the rounds in person, not because he feared that his orders might not be carried out, but because he thought the soldiers would do the work more willingly if their commander took his fair share. On this and on other occasions during the war he maintained discipline by appealing to his soldiers' honour, rather than by punishment. Many said he did this to increase his popularity. Others suggested that, accustomed as he was from childhood to a laborious life, he actually took pleasure in what other people call hardships. Be that as it may, he could not, by enforcing the most rigorous discipline, have served the state with more success or with more distinction.

At last, on the fourth day of the march, when the column was only a short distance from Cirta, scouts came hurrying in from all quarters at once. It was obvious that the Numidians were close at hand. But since the scouts came from different directions, and all agreed in reporting the approach of enemy forces, Marius could not tell on which front to form his battle-line. He therefore made no change in his formation but stayed where he was, prepared for an attack from any side. In this way he balked Jugurtha, who had divided his forces into four parts, feeling certain that as they all converged one or another of them could not fail to take the Romans in the rear. The enemy first made contact with Sulla, who, after speaking some words of encouragement to his cavalrymen, formed a part of them into tightly-packed squadrons and led them against the Moors. Meanwhile the rest of them stayed where they were, protecting themselves from long-range missiles and killing any of the enemy who came close. During this cavalry engagement Bocchus appeared with some infantry reinforcements brought by his son Volux – which, owing to a delay *en route*, had not taken part in the former battle – and attacked the Romans' rear line while Marius was busy in the front. For Jugurtha had brought his strongest division* against the Roman front. On hearing of Bocchus's arrival,

* The following narrative shows that this division consisted of cavalry.

however, he slipped away unseen, with a few followers, to join the latter's infantry. There, he shouted in Latin – which he had learnt to speak at Numantia – that it was useless for our men to continue the battle, as he had just killed Marius with his own hand. And he displayed the bloodstained sword with which, fighting bravely, he had killed some of the Roman infantrymen. This was a severe shock to our soldiers – though more because they were horrified at the idea than because they believed Jugurtha's assertion – while the natives were encouraged, and assailed their dismayed adversaries with even greater fury. The Roman resistance was almost broken when Sulla returned from routing his own opponents and charged the Moors in the flank. Bocchus instantly turned and fled. Jugurtha, while trying to keep his men in the field and to maintain his grasp on the victory he had so nearly won, was surrounded by our cavalry; all his comrades on both sides of him were slain, and he had to force his way out alone and escape as best he could from a hail of missiles. Meanwhile Marius, who after putting the enemy's cavalry to flight had heard that things were going badly in the rear, hastened up to the Romans' assistance. So the end of it was that the enemy were everywhere defeated. The broad plain presented a ghastly spectacle of flight and pursuit, slaughter and capture. Horses and men were thrown down; many of the wounded, without the strength to escape or the patience to lie still, struggled to get up, only to collapse immediately; as far as the eye could reach, the battlefield was strewn with weapons, armour, and corpses, with patches of bloodstained earth showing between them.

CHAPTER XII

THE BETRAYAL OF JUGURTHA (106–105 B.C.)

HAVING at last gained an indisputable victory, the consul completed his march to Cirta, his original objective. There, four days after the second defeat of the Barbarians, came envoys bringing a request from King Bocchus that Marius would send two absolutely reliable men to confer with him about a matter of importance both to Bocchus himself and to the Roman people. Marius immediately detailed Lucius Sulla and Aulus Manlius for this duty. Although they went at the king's invitation, they decided to take the initiative by making a statement themselves, hoping to change his purpose if his attitude was hostile, or to strengthen his desire for peace if he was that way inclined. Sulla was such an eloquent orator that Manlius, although he was the older man, let him act as spokesman. He briefly addressed the king, therefore, to the following effect:

'We rejoice greatly, King Bocchus, in view of your eminent qualities, that the gods have at last put it into your heart to choose peace rather than war, and, by refusing to contaminate your excellent character by association with the utter vileness of Jugurtha, to relieve us of the disagreeable necessity of meting out the same punishment to your errors as to his atrocious crimes. I may add that the Roman people have always preferred – even from those early days when they possessed nothing – to obtain friends rather than slaves, and have deemed it safer to rule by consent than by force. For you, no friendship is more advantageous than ours: in the first place, because the distance between us will minimize occasions of quarrel, while not diminishing the effectiveness of our support; secondly, because we already have plenty of subjects, whereas neither we nor anyone else ever had enough friends. I only wish you had adopted your present policy at first; for the benefits you would have received from the Roman people would assuredly have been many more than the injuries you have suffered as it is. However, since human destinies are controlled for the most part by Fortune, and since it seems to have been her pleasure that you should experience both our strong arm and our goodwill, seize the opportunity that she now offers you and go on as you have begun. You have many means ready to your hand of atoning for your errors by complying with our requirements. Finally, let me impress it upon you that there has never yet been a time when the Romans have allowed themselves to be outdone in generosity. I say nothing of what they can do in war: that, you have learnt by personal experience.'

To this address Bocchus made a temperate and friendly reply, which included a brief defence of his conduct. It was not out of hostility to Rome, he said, that he had taken up arms, but to protect his kingdom. For that part of Numidia from which he had forcibly expelled Jugurtha was his by right of conquest,* and he could not have been expected to let it be laid waste by Marius. Furthermore, the embassy which he had previously sent to Rome to ask for a friendly alliance had been rejected. However, he would say no more of what was past, and if Marius would give him leave he would now send another embassy to the Senate. But when leave was granted, the Barbarian was persuaded to change his mind by some of his friends whom Jugurtha had bribed. For the latter had heard about the mission of Sulla and Manlius, and, guessing what was afoot, was apprehensive of its consequences.

In the meantime Marius, after installing his army in its winter quarters, marched with his light infantry and

* Bocchus had not 'expelled' Jugurtha from any part of Numidia. Jugurtha had promised him a third part of his kingdom as the price of his help in driving out the Romans (section 97[2]).

part of the cavalry into the desert, to besiege a fort in which Jugurtha had placed all the Roman deserters to act as a garrison.

Bocchus now began once more to reflect on the two defeats he had sustained; perhaps, too, he sought the advice of some friends whom Jugurtha had omitted to bribe. At length he selected from among his courtiers five men of proved loyalty and sound intelligence. Their orders were to go first to Marius, and then, if they obtained his consent, to proceed as envoys to Rome; and they were given full powers to conclude a treaty of peace on any terms they could get. They set out promptly for the Roman headquarters, but on the way they were cut off and plundered by Gaetulian brigands, and fled, terror-stricken and in a sorry plight, to Sulla, whom the consul had left as propraetor when he started on his expedition. Instead of treating them as enemies and impostors, as their condition entitled him to do, Sulla received them with studied politeness and generosity, which made these Barbarians think that the Romans' reputation for avarice was undeserved. They could not doubt that a man who made them such magnificent presents was their friend. For in those days there were still many people who did not know that liberality might have ulterior motives, and imagined that anyone who was open-handed acted from sincere goodwill and that a present was a sure token of kindly feeling. So the envoys communicated to the quaestor the mission which Bocchus had entrusted to them, and asked him to help them with his favour and counsel, descanting upon the military might, integrity, and greatness of their king, and touching on other points which they thought would strengthen their case or conciliate their auditor. Sulla promised to do all they asked, and instructed them in what terms to address Marius, and in due course the Senate. They waited there some forty days.

When Marius, after achieving the object of his expedition,

returned to Cirta and was informed of the envoys' arrival, he sent for them and Sulla and also summoned Lucius Bellienus, governor of the Province, and all the senators then resident in any part of it. In their presence he received Bocchus's message. The envoys were given leave to proceed to Rome, and in the meantime they asked the consul to grant an armistice. This was approved by Sulla and most of the others; a few voted for adopting a haughtier attitude – ignorant, one may presume, of the instability of human fortunes and the constant vicissitudes to which they are subject. Having obtained all they asked for, three of the Moors started for Rome under the guidance of Gnaeus Octavius Ruso, a quaestor who had brought the soldiers' wages to Africa; the other two returned to the king, who heard all their news with pleasure – especially the kindly interest shown by Sulla. At Rome, the ambassadors begged the Senate to pardon the error into which their king had been led by Jugurtha's wickedness, and requested a friendly alliance. They received the following reply: 'The Senate and People of Rome do not forget either services or injuries. However, since Bocchus repents of his wrongdoing, they are willing to pardon him. As to friendship and alliance, he shall have these when he has earned them.'

When this message was delivered to Bocchus, he wrote to Marius asking for Sulla to be sent to him with full discretion to take such measures as he thought their common interest required. Sulla was accordingly sent, with an escort of horsemen and Balearic slingers; he also took with him some archers and a cohort of Paelignians* equipped with light armour, which allowed them to march at a good pace and yet protected them as well as heavier armour would have done against the light missiles used by the enemy. On the fifth day of their march Volux, the son of Bocchus, suddenly appeared in the

* The Paeligni lived in central Italy, some 70–80 miles east-north-east of Rome.

middle of the open plain. He had not more than a thousand cavalry with him; as they were not riding in ranks, however, but widely scattered, Sulla and his companions thought they were more numerous, and feared an attack. Each man therefore got ready for combat, checked his armour and weapons, and held himself alert. In spite of their alarming situation, they were inspired with hope by the recollection of the many victories they had gained over the foe who confronted them. Before long, some horsemen who had been sent forward to reconnoitre reported – as was indeed the case – that there was no sign of hostile activity.

As he came up, Volux called to Sulla, saying that he had been sent by his father to meet the Roman party and give them protection. For the rest of that day, and the next day, they proceeded together without fear. But in the evening, after they had encamped, the Moor suddenly ran to Sulla with an agitated, frightened look on his face, saying he had learnt from his scouts that Jugurtha was not far away, and earnestly begging Sulla to escape with him under cover of darkness. Sulla's pride would not entertain the idea. He had no fear, he said, of of a Numidian who had been soundly beaten so many times. He had confidence in his men's valour; but even if certain destruction threatened, he would stand his ground rather than betray his soldiers and disgrace himself by flight in order to prolong a life at best uncertain, and destined perhaps to be terminated ere long by disease. However, he accepted Volux's suggestion that they should leave the camp during the night, and at once ordered the soldiers to get their supper quickly, to light fires all over the camp, and to set out in silence at the first watch. After a fatiguing night march, a camp was being measured out, just at sunrise, when the Moorish horsemen reported that Jugurtha was encamped about two miles ahead. This news really terrified our men. They thought Volux had treacherously led them into a trap, and some said he ought to be executed out of hand and not allowed to commit such a crime with impunity.

Although Sulla shared their opinion, he prevented them from offering violence to the Moor and told them to be of good courage. 'Often before today,' he said, 'a few brave men have defeated a multitude. If it comes to a fight, the less you strive to avoid danger the safer you will be. No man who has weapons in his hands should expect help from his feet, which have nothing to defend him with. And however frightened you may be, you must never expose to the enemy the part of your body which is defenceless and blind.' He then accused Volux of practising against him as an enemy, and after appealing to great Jupiter to witness Bocchus's treachery and guilt, he bade the young man leave the camp. Volux begged him with tears not to believe such a thing. He declared there had been no double-dealing: it was all due to the cunning of Jugurtha, who had evidently used spies to discover the route they were following. 'However,' he said, 'since Jugurtha has not a large force with him, and since his hopes of obtaining men and supplies depend upon my father, I do not believe he will attempt any open violence while I am here to witness it. So I think our best course is to march boldly right through his camp. So far as I am concerned, my Moors can be either sent on in front or left where they are: I am prepared to go alone with you.' The situation being what it was, this proposal was adopted. They started at once, and since their unexpected arrival caught Jugurtha in two minds, they passed through unharmed while he hesitated, and a few days later reached their destination.

With Bocchus was a Numidian named Aspar, who spent much time in the king's company and was on familiar terms with him. Jugurtha had hastened to send him, on hearing of the proposed interview with Sulla, to act as his representative and to obtain private intelligence of Bocchus's plans. There was also with him a certain Dabar, a son of

Massugrada and a descendant of Masinissa; he was of inferior birth on his mother's side – for her father was the son of a concubine – but his many good qualities had greatly endeared him to the Moor. As he had found this man loyal to the Romans on many previous occasions, Bocchus forthwith sent him to tell Sulla that he was ready to carry out the wishes of the Roman people, and to suggest that Sulla himself should choose a day, place, and hour for a conference. 'Sulla need have no fear,' said Bocchus, 'of the envoy of Jugurtha; I have purposely avoided a premature rupture with him, so that Sulla and I can pursue our common interests with greater freedom: for there was no other means of guarding against his crafty schemes.' However, my information leads me to suspect that Bocchus was as treacherous as any Carthaginian could have been. Far from being actuated by the motive which he alleged, he had led on both the Roman and the Numidian by holding out hope of peace, and he many times pondered anxiously whether it was better to hand over Jugurtha to the Romans or Sulla to Jugurtha. He would have loved to betray us, but he could not summon up the courage.

In reply to Bocchus's message Sulla said he would say very little in front of Aspar, reserving all further discussion for a private interview, to which no one else, or at any rate as few persons as possible, must be admitted. He also told the king what answer to make to him before Aspar. When the preliminary meeting was held in accordance with Sulla's wish, he said the consul had sent him to ask Bocchus whether he intended to have peace or war. Bocchus replied, as instructed, by telling Sulla to return in ten days' time; he had still not come to any decision, he said, but would give his answer then. After this both parties withdrew to their camps. But in the middle of the night the king sent secretly for Sulla. Each was attended only by trustworthy interpreters; but Dabar was present as an intermediary, for his upright character made him acceptable to them both. Without any preliminaries Bocchus began as follows:

'Never did I think that I, the greatest king in Africa – the greatest indeed, so far as I know, in the world – should find myself indebted to a private individual. I swear that before I knew you, Sulla, I gave assistance to many, either in response to their requests or of my own accord, without myself needing any man's help. Such a loss of independence is to most people an occasion of grief, but I rejoice in it. To have come at last to stand in need of aid is the price I must pay for your friendship, which I value more highly than anything else in the world. It is open to you to test my sincerity in this. Arms, men, money – in a word, whatever I have that you desire – are yours to take and use. And as long as you live, never think that my debt of gratitude to you is discharged: it is one which I feel I can never begin to repay, and no wish of yours, if I know of it, shall remain unsatisfied. For to my mind it is less shameful for a monarch to be vanquished by arms than to be outdone in generosity.

'As regards the Roman commonwealth, whose interests you have been sent to protect, here briefly is what I have to say. I have not made war on the Roman people, nor have I at any time sought to involve them in war; I have only used arms to defend my frontiers against armed invaders. I will do so no longer, since that is what your countrymen wish. Conduct your war against Jugurtha as you please. I will not cross the River Muluccha, which was the boundary between Micipsa and myself, nor will I allow Jugurtha to retreat across it. If there is any further request that the Roman people can properly make of me, and that I can grant without loss of honour, it shall not be refused.'

Sulla's reply to this speech, in so far as it concerned him personally, was brief and modest; but on the subject of peace, and the common interests of Rome and Mauretania, he spoke at some length. Finally he made it clear to the king that he would not help himself by making fair promises: the Roman Senate and People, having shown themselves his superiors in arms, would not thank him for any such assurances. He must *do* something – and something that they could see was more to their advantage than to his own. 'And in fact', Sulla concluded, 'you need not look very far. You can easily lay hands on Jugurtha. If you hand him over to the Romans, they will be very greatly obliged to you. Friendship, alliance, the part of Numidia which you now claim – all will be yours without your lifting a finger.' The king at first refused, pointing out that ties of kinship and marriage – to say nothing of a formal treaty – bound him to Jugurtha, and adding that he was afraid lest by such treachery he might forfeit the loyalty of his own subjects, who liked Jugurtha and hated the Romans. But in the end, after much persuasion, he yielded, promising to do whatever Sulla wanted. They then took appropriate steps to make it appear that negotiations were in hand for concluding a peace, which the war-weary Jugurtha ardently desired. All was now arranged and the plotters went their separate ways.

On the following day the king summoned Aspar, Jugurtha's representative, and told him that Dabar had brought a message from Sulla to the effect that terms for a cessation of hostilities could now be discussed; accordingly, he must ascertain his master's views on the matter. Highly delighted, Aspar made his way to Jugurtha's camp; and after receiving full instructions from his king he travelled back post-haste, and, reaching Bocchus's headquarters on the eighth day, reported to him that Jugurtha was more than willing to comply with any demands that might be made, but that he distrusted Marius's intentions, since on several previous occasions a treaty concluded with a Roman general had been repudiated. 'If Bocchus wants', Jugurtha had said, 'to serve the interests of us both by securing a treaty of peace that will be honoured, let him arrange for all the interested parties to attend a conference – ostensibly for the purpose of discussing terms – and there deliver Sulla into my hands. When I have once got such an important man in my power, either the Senate or the People will soon conclude a formal treaty; for if so distinguished a man is taken prisoner through no fault of his own, while bravely serving his country, they will never be content to leave him in captivity.'

After prolonged deliberation the Moor at last undertook to do what Jugurtha asked. Whether his hesitation was real or assumed it is impossible to say; as a rule the headstrong impulses of kings are short-lived, and often they want today the opposite of what they wanted yesterday. Eventually, a rendezvous was appointed on a certain day for the peace conference, and in the meantime Bocchus summoned Sulla and Jugurtha's envoy by turns, giving each a friendly welcome and making the same promises to each, so that both of them were equally pleased and hopeful. On the night before the day fixed for the conference, the Moor first called his friends into counsel, then immediately changed his mind and dismissed them. Left alone, he pondered long and anxiously; and it is said that the expression on his face and the look in his eyes reflected the conflict by which his mind was harassed, and so, though no word passed his lips, revealed his innermost thoughts. At length, however, he summoned Sulla and agreed to his proposal that a trap should be set for the Numidian. When day came, it was reported that Jugurtha was close at hand. Attended by a few friends and by the Roman quaestor, Bocchus advanced to meet him, as though paying him a mark of respect, and took his stand on a small elevation that was clearly visible to the soldiers whom he had placed all round in concealment. The Numidian, with a large entourage, came to the same place – unarmed, according to agreement – and immediately, at a given signal, he was attacked by the ambush parties from every side at once. All his companions were slaughtered, and Jugurtha himself was put in irons and delivered up to Sulla, who conducted him to Marius.

About the same time the Gauls* inflicted upon our commanders Quintus Caepio and Gnaeus Manlius a defeat that made all Italy tremble with terror and inspired in the Romans a belief which persisted even to our own day – that while all other peoples could easily be subjected by their valour, a war against Gauls was a struggle for very existence and not just a matter of making a bid for glory. So when news came that the Numidian war was over and that Jugurtha was being brought to Rome in chains, Marius was re-elected consul in his absence and the province of Gaul was assigned to him. On the first day of January,† covered with glory and holding office as consul, he celebrated a triumph. At that time he was the one hope and resource of the state.

* By 'Gauls' Sallust means the Cimbri, a tribe of Germanic origin which had first migrated from the North Sea coast into central Europe, together with the Teutoni, and then, turning westwards, had overrun most of Gaul. The defeat took place at Arausio (modern Orange). Quintus Servilius Caepio, an Optimate opponent of Marius, was consul in 106; Gnaeus Manlius (more correctly, Mallius) Maximus, in 105.

† 104 B.C.

THE CONSPIRACY OF CATILINE

INTRODUCTION

MARIUS AND SULLA: THE SOCIAL WAR AND THE FIRST CIVIL WAR

THE forty-two years that elapsed between the Jugurthine war and the conspiracy of Catiline were full of turbulence and strife. There were serious external wars against the German invaders in the north and against Mithridates, king of Pontus in Asia Minor. At home, Rome's unjust treatment of her Italian allies goaded them into a desperate rebellion; there was a serious slave revolt; and the strife between political factions and rival leaders became so bitter that it ended in civil war and wholesale massacre. Sulla seized power as the first military dictator at Rome. The legions were now composed largely of landless men who volunteered for service and often served for long periods. As there were no money pensions, they looked to their commanders to reward them with plunder on active service and with allotments of land on demobilization. This naturally bound them to the commanders by an allegiance based on personal interest, which made it possible for a successful but unscrupulous general to use naked force in the furtherance of his own political aims or ambitions.

Marius was at the height of his fame in the closing years of the second century. He had not only changed the legionaries from short-term conscripts into semi-professional soldiers: he also made important changes in the organization of the army. The chief tactical units were henceforth the cohorts, ten of which – each with a nominal strength of six hundred men – made up a legion. By introducing improvements in equipment and training and by fostering a high *esprit de corps* in both legions and cohorts, Marius did much to increase the fighting efficiency of the armies. His defeat of the Cimbri and Teutoni in decisive battles at Aix-en-Provence (102) and near Vercelli in Piedmont (101), and the six consulships he held between 107 and 100, raised him to a position of such prestige that if he had possessed any statesmanlike qualities he could probably have effected valuable reforms in the social and political fields. Unfortunately he had little wisdom or even interest in these matters. His immediate concern was to secure allotments of land for the troops who had served with him in Africa and in the Northern campaigns; and for this purpose he supported the demagogue Lucius Appuleius Saturninus (tribune 103 and 100), who proposed a set of popular measures and prosecuted a bitter quarrel with the Optimate senators. But the illegalities and violent acts of Saturninus and his associate Gaius Servilius Glaucia (praetor 100) reached such a point that the Senate, by passing its 'last decree', called on Marius, then consul for the sixth time, to protect the state. He thereupon deserted the demagogues, who despite his efforts to save them were murdered by an angry mob. Thus the 'new man' who had reached such a pinnacle of fame and popularity by his military achievements proved a failure in politics. He and the popular leaders had tried to use one another for their own purposes; and now the Senate used him to defeat them.

Rome was comparatively quiet for the next few years. But serious trouble was brewing in Italy, because hardly anyone was willing to pay attention to the long-standing grievances of the Italian allies. For something like a century and a half, men from the various communities up and down the country had contributed their full share to Rome's success by supplying a considerable part of her soldiery. Yet, although a good many communities had by this time received either full citizenship or some of the rights of Roman citizens, the majority were still denied any such privileges. It was true that, in the absence of a representative system, few would have been able to use votes if they had had them. There were, however, social and legal advantages to be gained from citizen rights – for example, protection against acts of oppression on the part of magistrates and army officers. Apart from this, it was a matter of prestige and equity: they bitterly resented their exclusion because it was a gross injustice. A few wise statesmen had tried to remedy it. Marcus Fulvius Flaccus as consul in 125, Gaius Gracchus (122), and Marcus Livius Drusus as tribune in 91, had proposed legislation to that end, but failed in face of the conservatism of nearly all the senatorial leaders and the selfishness alike of businessmen and proletariat, who grudged the Italians a chance of sharing their privileges. Thus short-sighted prejudice prevented the question from ever being discussed on its merits. Drusus's failure in 91 was followed by the outbreak of the 'Italian' or 'Social' war. Almost all the 'Latin' communities, who already possessed some of the rights of citizenship, remained loyal; but nearly the whole of central Italy, and parts of the South, rose up in arms, mustering between them an army of 100,000. After some bitter fighting, this unnecessary and disgraceful war was brought to an end by the concession of the allies' demands – although means were devised at first to restrict the voting power of the newly enfranchised citizens.

The Italian question had been settled, but it was not long before calamity overtook Rome itself. Marius, if he was no statesman, was no violator of law and order – until, at the very end of his life, his character was perverted by resentment at his misfortunes and the evil example set by others. But his rival Sulla was both less scrupulous and more astute. In 106–5 his shrewd diplomacy had effected the capture of Jugurtha. He was a praetor in 93, but he had not yet done much to distinguish his career from that of other middle-aged Optimates. In 89, however, his successes in the Social war won him a consulship for the ensuing year, to be followed by a military appointment of the first importance: for he was to be governor of the Province of Asia and commander-in-chief in a war that was impending with Mithridates of Pontus. Unfortunately, a tribune of 88 named Publius Sulpicius Rufus, wanting apparently to secure Marius's support for a programme of measures that he had in hand, was unwise enough to attempt to have the Asiatic command transferred from Sulla to Marius. Sulpicius and Marius must have misunderstood Sulla's character. For they did not think it necessary to organize armed protection for themselves or for the state, and when Sulla marched on the city at the head of six legions which had been mustered for the coming war, it fell in a few hours. Sulpicius was soon killed; Marius escaped, making his way eventually to Africa.

Sulla had little time to spare at the moment. Mithridates had built up a formidable power in Asia Minor and Greece, and in 88 he irrevocably committed himself and most of the cities in the Province of Asia to war with Rome by organizing a cold-blooded massacre of the 80,000 Italian inhabitants of the Province. Landing in Greece in 87, Sulla defeated two of Mithridates's armies in 86; then, since his presence was urgently required in Rome, his enemies having got control of government and declared him a public enemy, he let off Mithridates with more lenient terms than he deserved and contented himself with severely punishing the rebellious Province.

Meanwhile, Sulla's enemies in Rome had seized control by methods as unconstitutional as his own, and even more ruthless. An able partisan of the Populares, Lucius Cornelius Cinna, secured appointment as consul each year from 87 to 84. When the Senate tried to depose him in 87, he and Marius, now returned from exile, occupied the city. Marius was now possessed by a bloodthirsty frenzy and massacred Sulla's supporters by the hundred, till Cinna was sickened by the carnage and turned his own troops on the cut-throats who were carrying it out. They declared themselves consuls for the year 86; but a few days after entering upon his seventh consulship Marius died. By his final acts of savagery, he had sullied a hitherto honourable record and disgraced the Popular cause in the eyes of all decent men. Later in the year Cinna sent a force to Greece in an attempt to wrest his command from Sulla, and in 84 he was preparing to go there himself with a fresh army when some of the troops mutinied and killed him.

In 83 Sulla landed at Brindisi with 40,000 men. Resistance to him was organized by Gnaeus Papirius Carbo (consul 85, 84, 82) and Gaius Marius the younger (consul 82), a son or adopted son of old Marius. The fighting, which was fierce, ended on 1 November 82 with the defeat of the last Marian army at one of the northern gates of Rome. In this campaign Sulla had the assistance of three able officers – Quintus Caecilius Metellus Pius, son of Metellus Numidicus who had commanded in the Jugurthine war; Marcus Licinius Crassus, who later became the richest man of his time and an influential politician (mentioned frequently in the *Catiline*); and Gnaeus Pompeius Magnus – Pompey the Great – who was destined to become the most powerful man in Rome and the most brilliant soldier of his day, till he was outshone by the even greater brilliance of Julius Caesar and defeated by him in the civil war of the early forties.

Sulla's victory was followed by massacres and proscriptions more horrible than any that had preceded them. The first list of victims included forty senators and 1,600 Equites, and the total number ran to several thousands. Allotments of land had to be found – by seizure from individual owners and by confiscation from towns, particularly those of Etruria and other northern districts, which had sided with the Marians – to accommodate 120,000 men from twenty-three demobilized legions. About the end of the year 82 Sulla was appointed dictator, 'to draw up laws and to settle the constitution of the Republic'. This office, which he held until he resigned it in 79, invested him with almost unlimited powers, not subject to veto or appeal, and enabled him to carry through a comprehensive programme of legislation. His main object was to restore the Senate to its former position of power and authority, and to render its control of affairs as secure as possible by curbing the forces which had threatened it in the past and might threaten it again – in particular, demagogic tribunes of the plebs and ambitious holders of high office, whether they were consuls in Rome or proconsuls in command of armies abroad. He enlarged the Senate by nominating 300 new members, and arranged for its numbers to be kept up in future by drafting into it annually the twenty men who had just held the office of quaestor* – the first step in a public career. Strict regulations were established about the age at which each magistracy could be held (forty-two was now fixed as the minimum age for the consulship), and a rule was made that no one should hold the same office a second time until ten years had elapsed. Each of the two consuls and the eight praetors† annually elected was required, after his term of office, to undertake the governorship of a province, normally for one year only. The powers of the tribunes were drastically curtailed: their right of veto was restricted, their right of initiating legislation in the Popular Assembly was taken away, and they were debarred from standing for any higher magistracy. Finally, Sulla reorganized the administration of criminal justice. Ever since the time of Gaius Gracchus,‡ Equestrian juries had continued to serve in the court which tried cases of extortion by provincial governors, and the same system was applied to the criminal courts instituted later for hearing charges of murder, embezzlement, treason, and electoral corruption. Sulla established two more

* Quaestors were either employed in Italy as receivers of revenue and paymasters, or attached to provincial governors or generals in the field, whom they assisted by discharging general administrative or military duties.

† The duties of praetors were mainly concerned with the administration of justice.

‡ With the exception of a period of about two years.

courts – for forgery and assault cases – and placed them all in the hands of senatorial jurors. Although the right of serving on these juries continued to be disputed between senators and Equites for the next ten years, this comprehensive system of criminal justice proved to be the most lasting part of Sulla's reforms. Most of the others, for various reasons, were soon swept away. The Senate lacked the political wisdom and foresight that would have enabled it to discharge properly the responsible duties laid upon it, because it still consisted too largely of Roman aristocrats and was not strengthened by the recruitment of able and experienced men from the Italian towns. Moreover, the Popular forces that opposed it, though they had been dealt a severe blow, soon recovered and renewed their attacks. Most serious of all, Sulla had failed to devise any effective check upon the power of successful generals. Less than ten years after his retirement, his own lieutenants Crassus and Pompey were using the threat of military force to put themselves in a position to destroy his constitution; and in another twenty years Julius Caesar invaded Italy at the head of a large army.

THE BREAKDOWN OF SULLA'S CONSTITUTION

To secure the restored supremacy of the Senate and prevent further attacks upon it by the Popular party, Sulla had relied mainly on his severe curtailment of the powers of the tribunes. Already in 75 B.C. the process of undoing his work had been begun, by the passing of a bill allowing ex-tribunes to stand for higher magistracies. As consuls in 70, Crassus and Pompey restored all the former rights and privileges of the tribunate.

With the object of lessening the political influence of the Equites, Sulla had put senators in charge of all the criminal courts. They were now deprived of this control by a measure providing that one third of the jurors should be senators, one third Equites, and the remaining third (probably) members of the propertied class ranking next below the Equites. Some senatorial juries had certainly abused their power. During the seventies there were at least two cases in which a verdict was clearly obtained by bribery, and others in which the acquittal of apparently guilty defendants aroused grave suspicion. Finally, when Gaius Verres, a governor of Sicily, was notoriously guilty of the most outrageous acts of plunder and oppression, he enlisted the support of such influential friends that in all probability it was only the exceptional energy and skill of Cicero, who prosecuted him, that prevented his securing an acquittal. These scandals could be held to justify the change that was now made; in effecting it, however, Pompey and Crassus may have been actuated largely by a desire to secure the support of the Equestrian financiers and businessmen, and it is doubtful if the mixed juries proved any more impartial than the senators had been.

Only two of Sulla's institutions now remained: first, the criminal courts themselves; second, the rules laid down for the tenure of the various magistracies and provincial governorships; and the latter were often set aside in favour of individuals – above all, in favour of Pompey himself. The Senate had proved too weak to retain a firm hold of the power that Sulla put back into its hands.

THE RISE OF CRASSUS AND POMPEY

Trouble with magistrates or ex-magistrates placed in command of armies started immediately after Sulla's retirement and kept recurring for many years. Unfortunately, there arose a series of emergencies that called for the services of good soldiers; and on each occasion either the Senate or the Assembly was persuaded, partly by real necessity and partly perhaps by nervous exaggeration of the danger, to authorize an extraordinary command. Already in 77 Marcus Aemilius Lepidus (consul 78), one of Sulla's army officers, threatened to march on Rome and frightened the Senate into passing its 'last decree' and declaring him a public enemy. Soon afterwards it was considered necessary to send a large army to Spain to fight against Quintus Sertorius, a Marian partisan who used his military genius and his compelling personality to make himself a popular ruler over the greater part of Spain, and for four years defied all the forces with which the Roman government opposed him. In 74 the continuing depredations of pirates necessitated the appointment of Marcus Antonius, father of Mark Antony the triumvir, to a special proconsular command, exercisable over all the Mediterranean; and in the same year a renewal of hostilities by Mithridates had to be met by the appointment of Lucius Licinius Lucullus to the governorship first of two and eventually of three eastern provinces. Meanwhile Italy was convulsed by a serious slave rising under the Thracian gladiator Spartacus, who raised a force of 70,000 men and in 72 actually defeated two consular armies.

To cope with these various emergencies three generals were available. Crassus was no more than a competent soldier; Lucullus was a brilliant strategist and administrator; Pompey proved no less able in administration and had the qualities of leadership that Lucullus lacked. Crassus, as proconsul in command of six legions, crushed Spartacus's revolt with ruthless efficiency. Although the holding of such commands in Italy was the very thing that Sulla had hoped to avoid in future, Crassus's appointment was constitutional, inasmuch as he was a senator of some ten years' standing and had just held a praetorship. The rapid advancement of Pompey, however, was unprecedented and highly irregular. In 83, at the age of twenty-three, he had raised three legions on his own initiative to fight for Sulla; in 82–79, with a special grant of *imperium* as propraetor, he defeated the Marians in Sicily and Africa, and on his return to Italy he kept his legions under orders and demanded a triumph, an honour which Sulla conceded in admiration of his audacity – or in fear of what he might do, since at that moment he was in a very strong position. In 77 he held a second propraetorian command against Lepidus, and kept his army mobilized until the Senate appointed him, as proconsul this time, to conduct the war in Spain against Sertorius – a hard-fought struggle which lasted over four years, and would have lasted even longer, had not Sertorius been assassinated by one of his own lieutenants.

Pompey reached home just in time to lend a hand in the final stage of the slave war and to rob Crassus of a part of the credit for winning it. Once again he was in no hurry to disband his troops (this seems to have been a regular technique of his), and he secured a second triumph, while Crassus had to be content with a much less coveted honour. All these powers had been entrusted to a man not yet thirty-five years old, who had held no ordinary magistracy; and he now came forward with a demand to be allowed to stand for the consulship of 70. Since Crassus also had a large army at his back, he could perhaps have prevented this unconstitutional proceeding on Pompey's part; but either from motives of personal interest or from patriotism – for if Pompey's ambition had been thwarted by the use of force, it might have meant another civil war – he chose to work with Pompey for the present, and the two of them were elected consuls for the year 70. Pompey was the first man in Roman history to become a consul before he was a senator.

Fortune continued to favour him. In 69–68 the pirates had grown so daring that they plundered the Italian coasts under the noses of Roman officials and were interfering with the city's corn supply. In 67 a tribune persuaded the Popular Assembly, in the teeth of senatorial opposition (Caesar is said to have been the only senator to support the proposal), to invest Pompey with a proconsular *imperium* valid over the whole of the Mediterranean sea and carrying authority equal to that of provincial governors for fifty miles inland, together with a large fleet and a large army, huge sums of money, and the right of appointing twenty-four legates. The judgement of the Assembly in this matter was quickly proved right. For more than thirty years the Senate had failed to do anything effective against the pirates; now the people's nominee cleared them off the seas in three months.

Meanwhile Lucullus, who since the end of 74 had been campaigning with great success against Mithridates and his son-in-law Tigranes of Armenia, had got into difficulties. The war had dragged on for more than six years; his soldiers were tired of serving in distant lands under a strict disciplinarian; and the Equites were annoyed by his statesmanlike action in relieving the Province of Asia from an intolerable load of debt to Roman financiers. In 66 a tribune carried a *lex Manilia* (supported by both Caesar and Cicero) adding to the powers already possessed by Pompey the command of all the Roman forces in Asia Minor. Mithridates's strength had been broken by Lucullus. Deserted by Tigranes and faced by revolts of his own subjects, the old king committed suicide in 63. Before leaving for home in 62, Pompey made the whole of the Near East secure, with a ring of coastal provinces and a number of client kingdoms to protect their eastern frontiers. Fifty cities were founded or restored, and the Roman revenues from Asia were increased by seventy per cent.

CATILINE

In the four orations that he delivered against Catiline in 63 B.C., and in an election speech in 64, Cicero portrays him as a monster of wickedness; and Sallust's picture of him is painted in almost equally lurid colours. There can be little doubt that their characterizations are substantially true. In the Sullan proscriptions he had shown himself not only a willing but a particularly bloodthirsty killer; and his conspiracy, despite his protestations of altruism, was in the main a reckless and selfish bid for lawless power, which, had it been successful even for the moment, must have resulted in a useless sacrifice of lives and in widespread misery – above all, for the poor citizens whom he professed to be trying to help.

Nevertheless, both Cicero and Sallust were admittedly under a temptation to exaggerate his vices and to omit the little that could be urged in his favour. Cicero's concern was to impress the Senate and the people with the enormity of Catiline's crimes in order to justify the measures which, as consul, he was taking or intended to take against him, and in order to enhance his own achievement in saving the Republic from the clutches of such a shocking criminal. Sallust had chosen the conspiracy as a theme because of its 'unprecedented iniquity' and the 'unprecedented danger' it caused: and being a writer with a keen sense of drama, it would not be surprising if he made the most of the iniquity and the danger by depicting its ringleader in an even worse light than the facts justified. Catiline's private life, though certainly profligate, was probably no worse than that of many of his contemporaries. His public career started respectably: he was elected praetor (68), and in the next year was entrusted with the government of the Province of Africa. At one time Cicero himself had some thought of defending him against a criminal charge, and even of supporting his candidature at the consular election in 64, in return for Catiline's support of his own candidature; and although this idea came to nothing, Catiline was in fact defeated only by a narrow margin. In a speech delivered some years later on behalf of a defendant who had once been closely associated with Catiline,* Cicero says that he was a strange mixture of evil and

* The speech in defence of Marcus Caelius Rufus (56 B.C.).

good: a man of enormous energy, a brave soldier, popular with a wide circle of friends to whom he was intensely loyal, generous both with his money and with his time. Indeed, Cicero freely admits that he himself once had a good opinion and high hopes of him, and that he was surprised and shocked by the discovery of his treason.

Up to the year 64, therefore, Catiline seems to have been merely an ambitious careerist who in spite of a taste for dissipation and homicide had something likable about him. What turned him into a dangerous revolutionary, apparently, was his failure to obtain a consulship. He was unable to stand in 66 and 65, because he was facing a charge of extortion in Africa. At the election of 64 he no doubt felt confident of success: he belonged to the aristocratic circle, and he was being supported by Crassus (which meant that he had plenty of money at his disposal for bribing electors), and probably by Caesar. His failure – by a small number of votes – must have been a bitter disappointment, especially as one of the successful candidates was Cicero, the first 'new man' in thirty years to become consul. At the election of 63 Catiline tried again. He had less chance of success this time, because he had three Optimate candidates standing against him and he had probably lost the support of Crassus and Caesar. What chance he had, he threw away by tactical errors – by uttering vague threats against the Establishment and the rich, and by announcing as his policy a general cancellation of debts, which, while it might attract the votes of Sullan veterans whose attempts at farming had landed them in bankruptcy and of spendthrift noblemen who were always in debt, was bound to alienate the support of the Equites, of small traders and farmers, and of the more respectable elements of the nobility. After his second defeat he threw common sense and caution to the winds and became a harebrained revolutionary. Besides his thwarted ambition, he was actuated by a bitter hatred of the consul

Cicero, who on both occasions had done all he could to ensure Catiline's defeat by attacking his character unmercifully and playing on the electors' fears of what might happen if he were elected.

RELATIONS OF CRASSUS AND CAESAR WITH CATILINE

During Pompey's absence abroad in the middle sixties, Crassus's wealth and rank placed him for a time in an influential position. But he does not appear to have had any particular policy or programme in view. His main motive was jealousy and fear of Pompey. Although they had co-operated closely during their joint consulship in 70 B.C., they were never on good terms personally. Crassus had good reason to be jealous of his younger colleague. In 82 he had done more than anyone else to help Sulla gain the victory that put him in control of Rome: yet it was the twenty-four-year-old Pompey who was granted a triumph by Sulla (for overcoming the Marian forces in Sicily and Africa). In 72–71 Crassus won the war against Spartacus: again, it was Pompey who triumphed – this time, for his victory in Spain over Sertorius. Now, in 67–66, Pompey had been chosen to hold the extraordinary commands against the pirates and Mithridates (these wars earned him a third triumph in 61); and all these honours had fallen to a man who never held any magistracy until he was elected consul six years before the legal age.

It was clear that when Pompey returned from the East he would be in a position of such overwhelming power that he could make himself master of the state if he chose. During his absence, therefore, Crassus made several efforts to increase his own political power; and he was aided in these attempts by Julius Caesar, who borrowed from him the large sums of money that he needed for the advancement of his own career. First Crassus tried to secure a foothold in Spain by getting a somewhat disreputable nominee, Gnaeus Calpurnius Piso, appointed governor; the appointment was made, but Piso was murdered by some Spaniards in 64.* Crassus next put forward a bill to annex the kingdom of Egypt and (probably) to send Caesar to take it over and organize it as a province; this was defeated by Cicero, acting in the interests of Pompey and the Optimates. A later proposal (64–63) was the establishment of a commission to acquire land for new colonies in Italy and in the provinces, the object being to obtain control of as much land as possible and thus put Crassus in a strong position for bargaining with Pompey, who would obviously need land for his veterans; this also was defeated by Cicero's opposition.

The relations of Crassus and Caesar with Catiline have been much debated, because the evidence about them is scanty and inconclusive. Crassus – and to some extent Caesar also, since they were co-operating at the time – was certainly believed by many of his contemporaries to have aided Catiline in some of his attempts to obtain power. This is very probable, for the reason adduced by Sallust:† 'Crassus, it was thought, would have been glad to see Pompey's supremacy threatened by the rise of another powerful man, whoever he might be.' He may well have thought it worth his while to help Catiline to a consulship: it might be very useful to have a daring and unscrupulous consul, under an obligation to Crassus for procuring his election and prepared to act in his interests. It is difficult to determine how deeply, and for how long, Crassus and Caesar were involved in Catiline's schemes. That either of them took any active part in the plot to murder the consuls on 1 January 65 is highly improbable: but Crassus certainly secured the appointment of Piso, one of the chief plotters, to a command in Spain; and the affair was hushed up by the Senate in a way that would hardly have been possible without

* See *Catiline*, sections 18, 19.

† Section 17[7].

the consent of Crassus, who was censor at the time, and of Caesar, who was aedile. One ancient authority states that they both did their utmost to secure Cicero's defeat at the consular election in the summer of 64 – which implies that they were working for his chief competitors, Catiline and Antonius. This, indeed, seems to be fairly certain. For Catiline and Antonius were handing out bribes on such a scandalous scale that the Senate tried to deter them by increasing the penalties for bribery; and since both of them were chronically in debt, the money must surely have come out of Crassus's pocket. The only argument against this view is the programme which, according to Sallust,* Catiline announced to his supporters shortly before the election: for this programme included the cancellation of debts and a proscription of the rich – the last measures likely to be approved by the millionaire Crassus. But the objection is not a fatal one. Crassus might well have been ready to disregard what Catiline was reported to have said in a private meeting of 'the neediest and most reckless' of his followers – confident that if he were really elected he could be kept under control. Alternatively, it is possible that Sallust, whose chronology is often confused, has transferred to the year 64 some parts of an election address which really belong to 63, when Catiline was again a candidate. This is made all the more likely by what he says about Catiline's activities between the two elections.† The statement that he was already, at that time, storing arms in depots throughout Italy and sending money to his lieutenant Manlius in Etruria – obviously for equipping and paying troops – is not confirmed by any other good authority, and seems improbable, in view of Cicero's repeated complaints, as late as November 63, that he could not induce either the people or responsible senators to believe in the existence of a serious conspiracy. It looks as if Sallust, either from inadvertence or to stress the

* Section 21. † Section 24.

heinousness of Catiline's guilt, has antedated his revolutionary plotting. He had such good reasons, however, for hating Cicero that we can well believe Cicero's statement that he made several attempts to kill him.*

There is no evidence that Crassus or Caesar supported Catiline at the election in 63, and it is unlikely that they did so. On this occasion, if not in the previous year, Catiline was certainly making reckless promises, involving something like national bankruptcy, which they could not have sanctioned. After his failure in the summer of 64, it must have seemed to Crassus very doubtful if he could ever get Catiline elected; and even if there was a chance of it, he could not now become consul until January 62. As to the accusation of direct complicity in the treasonable proceedings of 63, brought against Crassus by an obscure conspirator,† this suggestion, even if many believed it or half believed it at the time, is frankly incredible. If the conspiracy had by any chance succeeded, Crassus would almost certainly have been ruined. But there was in fact no chance of its succeeding: even if the plotters had been much stronger and much cleverer than they were (apart from Catiline himself they were incredibly careless and incompetent), any forces they could possibly muster would have been easily crushed by Pompey when he returned from the East.‡ If a really serious emergency had arisen, the Senate would have been forced to appeal to him to hurry back: thus Crassus, by involving himself in the movement, would have played straight into the hands of the rival whom he envied and disliked so much. The attempt of his enemies to charge Caesar with treasonable activities§ was even more absurd. In 63 he was elected to honourable and influential office as head of the state religion (*pontifex maximus*), and also to a praetorship for the following year, with a good hope of attaining a consulship three years

* *In Catilinam* I, sections 11, 15.

† See below, section 48. ‡ Section 39[4]. § Section 49.

later: in a position of such distinction and with such prospects before him, he would have been mad to mix himself up with Catiline's band of desperadoes, most of whom had not the intelligence to see that they were courting certain destruction.

THE PUNISHMENT OF THE CONSPIRATORS

There has been much controversy over the famous debate in the Senate on the punishment of Lentulus and the other four ringleaders of the plot, and their subsequent execution on Cicero's orders. Two points at least are tolerably certain. First, although Cicero, for obvious reasons, tried to shift the responsibility for the executions on to the Senate, it was in fact his own responsibility and not the Senate's: for the Senate was not a court of law empowered to pronounce sentence on any citizen. Second, if the Popular interpretation of the *senatus consultum de re publica defendenda* is accepted, as it is now by most scholars,* Cicero's action was in the strict sense illegal, in that it violated precise statutes, from obedience to which the Senate was not legally competent to absolve him; and by this illegality he rendered himself liable to subsequent prosecution. The Roman Republic had no means, such as modern states have in a declaration of martial law, of suspending the operation of the ordinary law in a crisis.

If this position is accepted, the real question is whether the circumstances justified Cicero's disregard of the laws protecting citizens against summary punishment. It has been argued, first, that death was a harsh and unjust penalty for the offences actually committed by the conspirators; second, that the executions were unnecessary: Cicero, it is said, was exaggerating the danger, and such danger as existed could have been met by less severe measures.

The argument of injustice is based on the fact that the plotters

* See above, pp. 23–4.

in Rome had not actually taken up arms or committed any acts of assassination or arson. There was indeed plenty of evidence of their intention to commit such acts: but, it is argued, intention is not performance, and only the performance could have deprived them of their rights as citizens and made them enemies of the state. Two answers can be made to this. Morally, it can be said that no valid distinction could be drawn between Catiline, whom everyone recognized as a public enemy because he was at the head of a private army (although that army had not yet raised a hand against anyone), and Lentulus, Cethegus, and the others, who were planning, by murder and incendiarism, to lay the city wide open to the attack of Catiline's army. Moreover, in the speech which he delivered on 9 November, Cicero had given them fair warning that not only treasonable acts, but any attempt thereat, would be severely dealt with.* On the practical grounds of public safety, the appropriate answer was given by Cato† in the debate on 5 December. After reminding the Senate that the prisoners had planned to make war on their country, he said: 'Other crimes can be punished when they have been committed, but with a crime like this, unless you take measures to prevent its being committed, it is too late; once it has been done, it is useless to invoke the law: when a city is captured, its defeated inhabitants lose everything.'

The question whether the executions were necessary or not must be considered in the light of the answers to two other questions: how serious was the danger, and what alternatives to the death penalty were available? It may be conceded that Cicero himself, in his speeches against Catiline, had strong motives for exaggerating the perils with which the state was threatened.‡ But Sallust, who as a partisan of Caesar had no reason to be prejudiced in Cicero's favour or to invent excuses

* *In Catilinam* II, section 27. † See below, section 52^{3-4}.

‡ See above, p. 162.

for his 'tyrannical' use of his authority, emphasizes the gravity of the situation. In section 50 he says there were plans on foot to rescue the prisoners by organizing gangs of their freedmen and clients, and even workmen and slaves; and he distinctly states that it was the discovery of these plans that caused Cicero to convoke the Senate and consult it as to what should be done with the accused. Evidently Sallust believed there was a serious possibility of a rescue. He makes Cato refer to it in another passage of his speech. Speaking of Caesar, who had proposed that the accused should be imprisoned in Italian towns, Cato says: 'No doubt he feared that if they remained in Rome either the adherents of the conspiracy or a hired mob might rescue them by force.' If they had regained their liberty, they might have been able to cause enough confusion and panic in Rome to give Catiline, who had an army in Etruria over 10,000 strong, a chance of marching on the city with some prospect of at least a temporary success. As it was, the executions had a very salutary effect: about two thirds of Catiline's troops immediately deserted him.* Considering the desperate resistance that he put up with the remainder, it is clear that this diminution of his strength must have saved the lives of many loyal Romans.

The question of an alternative punishment was rendered difficult by the peculiarities of the Roman penal system in the Republican period. Apart from the death penalty, which in practice was rarely inflicted on free men because condemned persons were generally allowed to go into voluntary exile, the only recognized penalties were fines, confiscation of property, loss of citizen rights, and in some cases banishment by a court sentence. There was no such thing as a sentence of imprisonment, the prison being used only as a place for temporary safe-keeping. It was largely this that made it so difficult to decide what to do in a case like that of Catiline's followers. Caesar's

* Section 57.

suggestion that they should be imprisoned for life* in Italian towns was even more contrary to custom than their summary execution: to Roman sentiment it would seem an intolerably severe punishment. Furthermore, it would have been impracticable. Even assuming that they could have been kept in safe custody for the time being – a doubtful assumption, in the absence of proper prisons and with so many of their sympathizers still at large – Cicero's term of office would expire in less than a month; and when he ceased to be consul, what guarantee was there that they would be held under lock and key? The Senate had no legal jurisdiction in such matters, and Cicero could not fetter his successors' freedom of action. Caesar himself recognized this difficulty, by his proposal that all future magistrates should be prohibited from raising the matter; but the Senate had no means of enforcing such a prohibition. The only alternative which might have been practicable would have been for Cicero to allow the prisoners to escape the death penalty by leaving the country immediately. That would have been in accordance with custom. But presumably he considered it too risky in the circumstances, and most historians think that he was probably right. In coming to this decision he was incurring a serious personal risk; and five years later his enemy Clodius drove him into temporary exile by a threat of prosecution, which Cicero did not care to face because in the political situation of 58 B.C. he could not have been sure of getting a fair hearing.

* It is almost certain that Caesar's proposal meant *life* imprisonment, although this has been disputed.

CHRONOLOGICAL SUMMARY

68 B.C. Catiline praetor.

67–66 B.C. Catiline propraetor in Africa; Pompey held proconsular command against the pirates (section 39).

66 B.C. Consuls: Manius Aemilius Lepidus, Lucius Volcatius Tullus (18); praetors: Marcus Tullius Cicero, Gaius Antonius; Pompey proconsul in Asia Minor (16, 17, 19, 39).

Summer: Publius Cornelius Sulla (18) and Publius Autronius Paetus (18, 47, 48[7]) elected consuls and unseated for bribery. Catiline returned from Africa; threatened with prosecution for extortion and prevented from standing for consulship at the second election (18).

5 December: Plot to assassinate the new consuls on 1 January (18).

65 B.C. Consuls: Lucius Aurelius Cotta, Lucius Manlius Torquatus (18); censors: Quintus Lutatius Catulus (34, 49), Marcus Licinius Crassus (17, 19, 48); curule aedile: Gaius Julius Caesar (49–51, 52[13–16], 54).

1 Jan.: Failure of plot to assassinate consuls (18).

5 Feb.: Failure of postponed murder plot (according to Sallust, 18).

Summer: Catiline again unable to stand for consulship on account of the extortion charge; subsequently acquitted.

64 B.C. Consuls: Lucius Julius Caesar, Gaius Marcius Figulus (17).

June: According to Sallust, Catiline started to plan

a revolutionary plot, to be carried out if he was elected consul for 63 B.C. (17, 20).

63 B.C. Consuls: Marcus Tullius Cicero (22–24, 26–29, 31, 36, 41, 43, 45, 48–49, 55), Gaius Antonius (21, 24, 26, 36, 56, 57[4–5], 59[4]); praetors: Publius Cornelius Lentulus Sura (one of the chief conspirators: 32, 39, 43, 44, 46, 47, 52[33], 55, 58[4]), Quintus Caecilius Metellus Celer (30, 42, 57), Quintus Pompeius Rufus (30), Lucius Valerius Flaccus (45, 46), Gaius Pomptinus (45); curule aedile: Publius Cornelius Lentulus Spinther (47); proconsuls: Quintus Caecilius Metellus Creticus (30), Quintus Marcius Rex (30, 32, 34); Marcus Petreius served as a legate under the consul Antonius in Etruria (59, 60); Julius Caesar elected pontifex maximus (49).

21 Oct.: Senate passed *senatus consultum de re publica defendenda* (placed too early by Sallust: 29).

27 Oct.: Gaius Manlius (24, 27, 28, 32, 33, 36, 59, 60) took up arms in Etruria (30).

6 Nov. (night): Meeting of conspirators at house of Marcus Porcius Laeca (placed too early by Sallust: 27).

7 Nov. (early morning): Attempted assassination of Cicero (28).

8 Nov.: Cicero's first speech against Catiline, in the Senate (31[6]);

(night): Catiline left Rome (32).

9 Nov.: Cicero's second speech against Catiline, to the people.

Mid Nov.: News of Catiline's arrival at Manlius's camp; the Senate declared Catiline and Manlius public enemies (36).

2 Dec. (night): Arrest of the conspirators' messengers at the Mulvian Bridge (45).

3 Dec. (morning): Evidence of the conspirators' guilt laid before the Senate by Cicero (46, 47).

(afternoon): Cicero's third speech against Catiline, to the people.

4 Dec.: Lucius Tarquinius's accusation of Crassus in the Senate (48); rewards voted to the Allobroges and Titus Volturcius (50); attempted rescue of the conspirators (50).

5 Dec.: Debate in Senate on punishment of the conspirators (50–53); Cicero's fourth speech against Catiline, in the Senate during the debate.

(evening): Execution of the conspirators (55).

62 B.C. Consuls: Decimus Junius Silanus (50, 51^{16-24}), Lucius Licinius Murena; praetor: Gaius Julius Caesar; tribunes of the plebs: Marcus Porcius Cato (52–54), Lucius Calpurnius Bestia (a supporter of Catiline: 17^{3}, 43^{1}); proconsuls: Gaius Antonius (appointed to Province of Macedonia, but temporarily commanding against Catiline in N. Italy: 57^{4-5}, 59^{4}), Quintus Caecilius Metellus Celer (Cisalpine Gaul; also acting against Catiline: 57); Marcus Petreius served as a legate under Antonius (59, 60).

January (?): Defeat and death of Catiline at Pistoia (57–61).

CHAPTER I

PREFACE

EVERY man who wishes to rise superior to the lower animals should strive his hardest to avoid living all his days in silent obscurity, like the beasts of the field, creatures which go with their faces to the ground and are the slaves of their bellies. We human beings have mental as well as physical powers; the mind, which we share with gods, is the ruling element in us, while the chief function of the body, which we have in common with the beasts, is to obey. Surely, therefore, it is our intellectual rather than our physical powers that we should use in the pursuit of fame. Since only a short span of life has been vouchsafed us, we must make ourselves remembered as long as may be by those who come after us. Wealth and beauty can give only a fleeting and perishable fame, but intellectual excellence is a glorious and everlasting possession.

Yet it was long a subject of hot dispute among men whether physical strength or mental ability was the more important requirement for success in war. Before you start on anything, you must plan; when you have made your plans, prompt action is needed. Thus neither is sufficient without the aid of the other.

Accordingly the world's first rulers, who were called kings, adopted one or other of two different policies, seeking either to make the most of their intellectual endowment or to develop their bodily strength. In those days men had not yet learnt to be covetous: each was content with what he had. It was only when Cyrus* in Asia and the Spartans and Athenians in Greece began to bring cities and nations into subjection, and to engage in wars because they thirsted for power and thought their glory was to be measured by the extent of their

* King of Persia 559–529 B.C.

dominions, that the test of experience decided the ancient controversy: brains were shown to be more important than brawn. It is a pity that kings and rulers do not apply their mental powers as effectively to the preservation of peace as to the prosecution of war. If they did, human life would be less chequered and unstable than it is: we should not see everything drifting to and fro in change and confusion. Sovereignty can easily be maintained by the same qualities as enable a man to acquire it. But when idleness replaces industry, when self-restraint and justice give place to lust and arrogance, the moral deterioration brings loss of station in its train. A degenerate ruler is always supplanted by a better man than himself.

Success in agriculture, seafaring, or building always depends on human excellence. But many are the men who, slaves of gluttony and sloth, have gone through life ignorant and uncivilized, as if they were mere sojourners in a foreign land, reversing, surely, the order of nature by treating their bodies as means of gratification and their souls as mere encumbrances. It makes no odds, to my mind, whether such men live or die; alive or dead, no one ever hears of them. The truth is that no man really lives or gets any satisfaction out of life, unless he devotes all his energies to some task and seeks fame by some notable achievement or by the cultivation of some admirable gift.

The field is wide, and men follow their natural bent in choosing this path or that. It is noble to serve the state by action, and even to use a gift of eloquence on its behalf is no mean thing. Peace, no less than war, offers men a chance of fame: they can win praise by describing exploits as well as by achieving them. And although the narrator earns much less renown than the doer, the writing of history is, in my opinion, a peculiarly difficult task. You must work hard to find words worthy of your subject. And if you censure misdeeds, most people will accuse you of envy and malice. When you write of the outstanding merit and glory of good men, people are quite ready to accept what they think they could easily do themselves; but anything beyond that is dismissed as an improbable fiction.

My earliest inclinations led me, like many other young men, to throw myself wholeheartedly into politics. There I found many things against me. Self-restraint, integrity, and virtue were disregarded; unscrupulous conduct, bribery, and profit-seeking were rife. And although, being a stranger to the vices that I saw practised on every hand, I looked on them with scorn, I was led astray by ambition and, with a young man's weakness, could not tear myself away. However much I tried to dissociate myself from the prevailing corruption, my craving for advancement exposed me to the same odium and slander as all my rivals.

After suffering manifold perils and hardships, peace of mind at last returned to me, and I decided that I must bid farewell to politics for good. But I had no intention of wasting my precious leisure in idleness and sloth, or of devoting my time to agriculture or hunting – tasks fit only for slaves. I had formerly been interested in history, and some work which I began in that field had been interrupted by my misguided political ambitions. I therefore took this up again, and decided to write accounts of some episodes in Roman history that seemed particularly worthy of record – a task for which I felt myself the better qualified inasmuch as I was unprejudiced by the hopes and fears of the party man.

It is my intention to give a brief account, as accurate as I can make it, of the conspiracy of Catiline, a criminal enterprise which I consider specially memorable as being unprecedented in itself and fraught with unprecedented dangers to Rome. I must preface my narrative by a short description of Catiline's character.

Lucius Catiline was of noble birth. He had a powerful intellect and great physical strength, but a vicious and depraved nature. From his youth he had delighted in civil war, bloodshed, robbery, and political strife, and it was in such occupations that he spent his early manhood. He could endure hunger, cold, and want of sleep to an incredible extent. His mind was daring, crafty, and versatile, capable of any pretence and dissimulation. A man of flaming passions, he was as covetous of other men's possessions as he was prodigal of his own; an eloquent speaker, but lacking in wisdom. His monstrous ambition hankered continually after things extravagant, impossible, beyond his reach. After the dictatorship of Lucius Sulla, Catiline had been possessed by an overmastering desire for despotic power, to gratify which he was prepared to use any and every means. His headstrong spirit was tormented more and more every day by poverty and a guilty conscience, both of which were aggravated by the evil practices I have referred to. He was incited also by the corruption of a society plagued by two opposite but equally disastrous vices – love of luxury and love of money.

Since I have had occasion to mention public morality, it seems appropriate to go back further and briefly describe the principles by which our ancestors guided their conduct in peace and war, their method of governing the state which they made so great before bequeathing it to their successors, and the gradual degeneration of its noble character into vice and corruption.

The city of Rome, as far as I can make out, was founded and first inhabited by Trojan exiles who, led by Aeneas, were wandering without a settled home, and by rustic natives who lived in a state of anarchy uncontrolled by laws or government. When once they had come to live together in a walled town, despite different origins, languages, and habits of life, they coalesced with amazing ease, and before long what had been a heterogeneous mob of migrants was welded into a united nation.

When however, with the growth of their population, civilization, and territory, it was seen that they had become powerful and prosperous, they had the same experience as most people have who are possessors of this world's goods: their wealth aroused envy. Neighbouring kings and peoples attacked them, and but few of their friends aided them; the rest were scared at the prospect of danger and held aloof. The Romans, however, were alert both at home and abroad. They girded themselves in haste and with mutual encouragement marched forth to meet their foes, protecting by force of arms their liberty, country, and parents. Then, after bravely warding off the dangers that beset them, they lent aid to their allies and friends, and made new friends by a greater readiness to render services than to accept help from others.

Their government was a constitutional monarchy. Picked men, in whom the physical weakness of age was compensated by outstanding wisdom, formed a council of state, and were called 'Fathers', either on account of their age or because their duties resembled those of the father of a family. In course of time the monarchy, which originally had served to safeguard liberty and enhance the prestige of the state, degenerated into an oppressive despotism. Thereupon they instituted a new régime in which authority was divided between two annually elected rulers;* this limitation of their power, it was thought, would prevent their being tempted to abuse it.

It was in this period that individuals were first able to distinguish themselves and display their talents to greater advantage; for kings are more suspicious of good men than of bad, and always fear men of merit. Indeed, it almost passes belief what rapid progress was made by the whole state when once it had gained its liberty; such was the desire for glory that had possessed men's hearts. Young men no sooner reached the age

* Traditionally in 510 B.C.; these are the magistrates who in the following century began to be called consuls.

when they were fit for military service than they went to camp and learnt the art of soldiering in the school of laborious experience, taking more delight in costly armour and chargers than in loose women or the pleasures of the table. To such men no toil came amiss, no ground was too steep or rugged, no armed foe formidable; courage had taught them to overcome all obstacles. To win honour they competed eagerly among themselves, each man seeking the first opportunity to cut down an enemy or scale a rampart before his comrades' eyes. It was by such exploits that they thought a man could win true wealth – good repute and high nobility. Their thirst for glory, and ever more glory, was insatiable; as for money, their only ambition was to come by it honourably and spend it openhandedly. I could mention places where vast enemy hosts were routed by a handful of Romans, and towns of great natural strength that they took by assault. But I must not digress too far from my proper theme.

There can be no question that Fortune is supreme in all human affairs. It is a capricious power, which makes men's actions famous or leaves them in obscurity without regard to their true worth. I do not doubt, for instance, that the exploits of the Athenians were splendid and impressive; but I think they are much overrated. It is because she produced historians of genius that the achievement of Athens is so renowned all the world over; for the merit of successful men is rated according to the brilliance of the authors who extol it. The Romans never had this advantage, because at Rome the cleverest men were also the busiest. No one was a thinker without being a man of action as well. Their leading citizens preferred deeds to words, and chose rather to do something that others might justly praise than merely to tell of what others did.

In peace and war, as I have said, virtue was held in high esteem. The closest unity prevailed, and avarice was a thing almost unknown. Justice and righteousness were upheld not so much by law as by natural instinct. They quarrelled and fought with their country's foes; between themselves the citizens contended only for honour. In making offerings to the gods they spared no expense; at home they lived frugally and never betrayed a friend. By combining boldness in war with fair dealing when peace was restored, they protected themselves and the state. There are convincing proofs of this. In time of war, soldiers were often punished for attacking against orders or for being slow to obey a signal of recall from battle, whereas few ever ventured to desert their standards or to give ground when hard pressed. In peace, they governed by conferring benefits on their subjects, not by intimidation; and when wronged they would rather pardon than seek vengeance.

Thus by hard work and just dealing the power of the state increased. Mighty kings were vanquished, savage tribes and huge nations were brought to their knees; and when Carthage, Rome's rival in her quest for empire, had been annihilated,* every land and sea lay open to her. It was then that fortune turned unkind and confounded all her enterprises. To the men who had so easily endured toil and peril, anxiety and adversity, the leisure and riches which are generally regarded as so desirable proved a burden and a curse. Growing love of money, and the lust for power which followed it, engendered every kind of evil. Avarice destroyed honour, integrity, and every other virtue, and instead taught men to be proud and cruel, to neglect religion, and to hold nothing too sacred to sell. Ambition tempted many to be false, to have one thought hidden in their hearts, another ready on their tongues, to become a man's friend or enemy not because they judged him worthy or unworthy but because they thought it would pay them, and to put on the semblance of virtues that they had not. At first these vices grew slowly and sometimes met with punishment; later on, when the disease had spread like a plague, Rome changed:

* In 146 B.C.

her government, once so just and admirable, became harsh and unendurable.

At first, however, it was not so much avarice as ambition that disturbed men's minds – a fault which after all comes nearer to being a virtue. For distinction, preferment, and power are the desire of good and bad alike – only, the one strives to reach his goal by honourable means, while the other, being destitute of good qualities, falls back on craft and deceit. Avarice is different: it means setting your heart on money, a thing that no wise man ever did. It is a kind of deadly poison, which ruins a man's health and weakens his moral fibre. It knows no bounds and can never be satisfied: he that has not, wants; and he that has, wants more. After Sulla had used armed force to make himself dictator, and after a good beginning turned out a bad ruler,* there was universal robbery and pillage. One man coveted a house, another an estate; and the victors behaved without restraint or moderation, committing foul and inhuman outrages against their fellow citizens. To make matters worse, Sulla had sought to secure the loyalty of the army he commanded in Asia by allowing it a degree of luxury and indulgence that would not have been tolerated by his predecessors, and the pleasures they enjoyed during leisure hours in those attractive lands soon enervated the men's warlike spirit. It was there that Roman soldiers first learnt to indulge in wine and women, and to cultivate a taste for statues, pictures, and embossed plate, which they stole from private houses and public buildings, plundering temples and profaning everything sacred and secular alike. When victory was won, as might be expected of such troops, they stripped their enemy bare. Since even philosophers cannot always resist the temptations of success, how should these demoralized men show restraint in their hour of triumph?

As soon as wealth came to be a mark of distinction and an

* See Introduction, p. 155.

easy way to renown, military commands, and political power, virtue began to decline. Poverty was now looked on as a disgrace and a blameless life as a sign of ill nature. Riches made the younger generation a prey to luxury, avarice, and pride. Squandering with one hand what they grabbed with the other, they set small value on their own property while they coveted that of others. Honour and modesty, all laws divine and human, were alike disregarded in a spirit of recklessness and intemperance. To one familiar with mansions and villas reared aloft on such a scale that they look like so many towns, it is instructive to visit the temples built by our godfearing ancestors. In those days piety was the ornament of shrines; glory, of men's dwellings. When they conquered a foe, they took nothing from him save his power to harm. But their base successors stuck at no crime to rob subject peoples of all that those brave conquerors had left them, as though oppression were the only possible method of ruling an empire. I need not remind you of some enterprises that no one but an eyewitness will believe – how private citizens have often levelled mountains and paved seas for their building operations. Such men, it seems to me, have treated their wealth as a mere plaything: instead of making honourable use of it, they have shamefully misused it on the first wasteful project that occurred to them. Equally strong was their passion for fornication, guzzling, and other forms of sensuality. Men prostituted themselves like women, and women sold their chastity to every comer. To please their palates they ransacked land and sea. They went to bed before they needed sleep, and instead of waiting until they felt hungry, thirsty, cold, or tired, they forestalled their bodies' needs by self-indulgence. Such practices incited young men who had run through their property to have recourse to crime. Because their vicious natures found it hard to forgo sensual pleasures, they resorted more and more recklessly to every means of getting and spending.

CHAPTER II

CATILINE'S FIRST ATTEMPTS AT REVOLUTION

AMID the corruption of the great city Catiline could easily surround himself, as with a bodyguard, with gangs of profligates and criminals. Debauchees, adulterers, and gamblers, who had squandered their inheritances in gaming-dens, pot-houses, and brothels; anyone who had bankrupted himself to buy impunity for his infamous or criminal acts; men convicted anywhere of murder or sacrilege, or living in fear of conviction; cut-throats and perjurers, too, who made a trade of bearing false witness or shedding the blood of fellow citizens; in short, all who were in disgrace or afflicted by poverty or consciousness of guilt, were Catiline's intimate associates. And if anyone as yet innocent happened to become friendly with him, the temptations to which daily intercourse with Catiline exposed him soon made him as evil a ruffian as the rest. It was above all the young whose intimacy he sought; their minds, being still impressionable and changeable, were easily ensnared. In order to gratify the youthful desires of each, he procured mistresses for some, bought dogs and horses for others, and spared neither his purse nor his honour to put them under obligations and make them his faithful followers. Some,* I know, have believed that the young men who resorted to Catiline's house practised unnatural lewdness; but this rumour was credited rather because the rest of their conduct made it seem a likely inference than because anyone knew it to be so. For one thing, Catiline had in his early days engaged in many scandalous intrigues – one with a maiden of noble birth, another with a priestess of Vesta, not

* Among these was Cicero – if he really believed the assertions to that effect which he made in his speeches against Catiline.

to mention similar offences against law and morality. He ended by falling in love with Aurelia Orestilla, a woman in whom no respectable man ever found anything to praise except her beauty, and it is generally accepted as a fact that when she hesitated to marry him because she was afraid of his grown-up son by a previous marriage, he murdered his son in order to clear the house of an impediment to this unhallowed union. Indeed, I think it was principally this deed that determined him to postpone his criminal attempt no longer. His unclean mind, hating god and fellow man alike, could find rest neither waking nor sleeping: so cruelly did remorse torture his frenzied soul. His complexion was pallid, his eyes hideous, his gait now hurried and now slow. Face and expression plainly marked him as a man distraught.

To the youths he had entrapped in the way I have described, he taught many kinds of wickedness. From their ranks he would provide men to commit perjury or to affix their seals to a forged document. He thought nothing of damaging their credit and their fortunes or of exposing them to peril; then, having ruined their reputations and stripped them of all sense of shame, he made bigger demands upon them. Even if he had no immediate motive for wrongdoing, he caused inoffensive persons to be attacked or killed with as much malevolence as if they had been guilty of injuring him. Rather than allow his pupils to lose their skill or nerve through lack of practice, he would have them commit needless outrages.

With such friends and allies to rely on, with the whole empire bankrupt and most of Sulla's veterans, ruined by extravagant living, looking back regretfully to the loot which past victories had brought them and longing for civil war, Catiline planned a revolution. There were no troops in Italy, and Pompey was fighting in far distant lands.* Catiline himself

* Against Mithridates, king of Pontus; see Introduction, p. 161.

had high hopes of being elected consul. The Senate suspected nothing and everything seemed quiet and secure – which gave him just the opportunity he wanted. About the beginning of June, therefore, in the consulship of Lucius Caesar and Gaius Figulus,* he began by making overtures to individuals, encouraging some, sounding others, and pointing out to them his own resources, the unprepared condition of the state, and the attractive prizes that a conspiracy offered. When he was satisfied with the results of his inquiries, he convened a general meeting of the neediest and most reckless of his acquaintance. It was attended by the senators Publius Lentulus Sura, Publius Autronius, Lucius Cassius Longinus, Gaius Cethegus, Publius and Servius Sulla the sons of Servius Sulla, Lucius Vargunteius, Quintus Annius, Marcus Porcius Laeca, Lucius Bestia, and Quintus Curius; by Marcus Fulvius Nobilior, Lucius Statilius, Publius Gabinius Capito, and Gaius Cornelius, members of the Equestrian Order; and by many members of the local nobility from Italian 'colonies'† and municipalities.‡ There were also a number of men of high standing who took a more secret part in the movement, influenced more by the hope of gaining power than by poverty or any other necessity. Indeed the Roman youth in general, especially those of high rank, looked with favour on Catiline's enterprise. Although they had the means, without stirring a finger, to live in splendour, or, if they so desired, in luxurious ease, they preferred a chance to a certainty and chose war

* 64 B.C.

† i.e. Italian towns founded by groups of Roman citizens, or existing towns to which groups of Roman citizens were sent. The earliest colonies were founded for strategic purposes on the Italian coasts. Later, colonies were granted powers of local government, and began to be founded for social and political reasons – to provide for needy citizens or veteran soldiers. Overseas colonies were very few during the Republican period.

‡ At this date, the term *municipia* included all Italian towns possessing local autonomy, with the exception of *coloniae*. In addition to their local franchise, their inhabitants now had Roman citizenship.

instead of peace. There were some who believed at the time that Marcus Licinius Crassus also was aware of the design. His hated rival Pompey was at the head of a great army, and Crassus, it was thought, would have been glad to see Pompey's supremacy threatened by the rise of another powerful man, whoever he might be, fully confident that if the conspirators succeeded he would readily be accepted as their leader.

First, however, I must mention a similar plot which Catiline and a few others had previously formed against the state. I will give as accurate an account of it as I can. In the consulship of Lucius Tullus and Manius Lepidus,* the consuls elect, Publius Autronius and Publius Sulla, had been prosecuted and punished under the laws against electoral corruption. Shortly afterwards Catiline was prevented from standing for one of the vacant consulships, because he was on trial for extortion and so could not enter his name within the specified number of days.† About the same time a needy young noble called Gnaeus Piso, a faction-fighter of reckless daring, was being goaded into a revolutionary intrigue by his poverty and unprincipled character. To this man Catiline and Autronius revealed their plans in the first week of December: they were plotting to assassinate the new consuls Lucius Cotta and Lucius Torquatus in the Capitol on the first of January,‡ to seize the consular fasces for themselves, and to send Piso with an army to occupy the two Spanish provinces. Because their murderous intent was discovered, they postponed its execution till the fifth of February, and this time they planned to destroy most of the senators as well as the consuls. Had not Catiline

* 66 B.C.

† Sallust is mistaken in saying that Catiline was actually on trial at this time: Cicero's references to the affair make it clear that the trial did not take place until the summer of 65. But the impending prosecution would provide the presiding consul with a reason for refusing to accept Catiline's candidature, and there is some evidence that this is what happened.

‡ 65 B.C.

been in too great a hurry to give the signal to his accomplices in front of the Senate House, that day would have seen the commission of the most heinous crime in the annals of Rome. As it was, the armed conspirators had not yet mustered in force; so the plan failed.* Piso was afterwards sent as quaestor with praetorian powers to Eastern Spain. His appointment was strongly urged by Crassus, because he knew Piso to be a bitter enemy of Pompey. At the same time the Senate was quite willing to assign him the province, since they were glad to remove such an unprincipled character to a distance from Rome. Moreover many good citizens thought he would be a protection against the already formidable power of Pompey. Piso was killed, in the course of a journey through his province, by some Spanish horsemen who formed part of his army. Some say that the natives could not tolerate the injustice, arrogance, and cruelty of his conduct as governor. Others maintain that the horsemen were old and devoted retainers of Pompey and were set on by him to attack Piso: they point out that the Spaniards never committed any other such crime and had patiently endured much oppression. I shall leave this point open and shall say no more about this earlier conspiracy.

When Catiline had assembled the men whom I mentioned,† although he had often had long conferences with each of them individually, he thought it advisable to address an exhortation to the whole company. Accordingly he made them withdraw into a remote part of the house and, after excluding all witnesses, spoke to the following effect:

'Were I not assured of your courage and loyalty, I could not use this favourable opportunity that fortune has vouchsafed me. However high our hopes, however easy it might have seemed for us to seize power, all would have been in vain. For with only cowards or triflers to rely on, I for one would not

* Neither Cicero nor any other writer mentions this second attempt.

† See above, section 17; Sallust now reverts to the events of 64 B.C.

throw away a certainty to grasp at a hazardous chance. It is because I have found you brave and faithful to me on many important occasions, that I venture to embark on a great and noble enterprise; also because I have observed that what seems good or bad to me seems so to you: for identity of likes and dislikes is the one solid foundation of friendship.

'The projects which I have been turning over in my mind have already been explained to each of you separately. But for my own part, every passing day kindles my enthusiasm more and more when I think what will be our lot unless we ourselves assert our claim to liberty. Ever since the state came under the jurisdiction and control of a powerful oligarchy, it is always they who receive tribute from foreign kings and princes and rake in taxes from every people and tribe. The rest of us, however energetic and virtuous we may be, whether our birth be noble or base, are but a crowd of nobodies without influence or authority, subservient to men who in a soundly governed state would stand in awe of us. Thus all influence, power, office, and wealth are in their hands or where they choose to bestow them; all they leave for us is danger, defeat, prosecutions, and poverty. How long, brave comrades, will you endure it? Is it not better to die courageously and have done with it, than to drag out lives of misery and dishonour as the playthings of other men's insolence, until we lose them ignominiously in the end? But in truth – I call on gods and men to witness it – victory is within our grasp. We have the strength of youth and we have stout hearts, whereas our opponents are enfeebled by age and soft living. We have but to make a start: the rest will follow easily. Can anyone who has the spirit of a man endure that they should have a superfluity of riches to waste in building out into the sea and levelling mountains, while we lack means to buy necessities? They have two, three, or four houses joined together, when we have not a home to call our own. Though they buy pictures, statues, and vessels of chased metal, though they pull down new houses to build others, laying waste their wealth and making inroads upon it in every imaginable way, yet all their extravagance cannot exhaust it. For us there is destitution at home and debts everywhere else; misery now, and a still worse future to look forward to; we have nothing left, in fact, save the breath we draw in our wretchedness.

'Awake, then! Here, here before your eyes, is the liberty that you have often yearned for, and withal affluence, honour, and glory, all of which fortune offers as the prizes of victory. Consider your situation and your opportunity, the peril and want that beset you, and the rich spoils that may be won in war: these plead more strongly than any words of mine. Use me as your commander or as a soldier in the ranks: my heart and my hands shall be at your service. These are the objects I hope to help you achieve when I am your consul – unless indeed I deceive myself and you are content to be slaves instead of masters.'

This speech was addressed to men who were afflicted with manifold misfortunes and had nothing good to enjoy or to hope for; and to them the disturbance of the peace was in itself a highly attractive proposition. Most of them, however, asked Catiline to explain on what lines he intended to conduct the war, what were the prizes they would be fighting for, and what help they could count on or might hope to obtain from various quarters. Thereupon Catiline promised them the cancellation of debts and a proscription of the rich; magistracies and priesthoods; opportunities of plunder, and all the other desirable things with which war satisfies the greed of victors. In Eastern Spain, he added, was Piso; in Mauretania, Publius Sittius of Nocera* at the head of an army – both of them accomplices in the plot. Moreover, one of the consular candidates was Gaius Antonius,† whom he hoped to have as his

* A town in Campania, north-west of Salerno. † Uncle of Mark Antony.

colleague in that office; and since Antonius, besides being his intimate friend, was in desperate straits, he could count on his co-operation when, as consul, he began to execute his plans. Then he proceeded to heap abuse on all honest citizens, and, praising each of his adherents by name, reminded them either of their needy condition or of their ambitions, of the prosecutions that threatened them or the disgrace they had incurred, of Sulla's victory and the spoil with which it had enriched them. All were now thoroughly roused; whereupon, after an urgent appeal for their help at the forthcoming election, he dismissed the meeting. There was a rumour current at the time that when Catiline, on the conclusion of his speech, called on the associates of his plot to swear an oath, he passed round bowls of human blood mixed with wine; and when all had tasted of it after invoking a curse upon themselves if they broke faith, in accordance with the usual practice at such solemn ceremonies, he revealed the details of his scheme. This he is said to have done in order that the consciousness of having jointly participated in such an abomination might make them more loyal to one another. Others however thought that this story, like many others, was invented by people who believed that the odium which afterwards arose against Cicero could be lessened by imputing hideous crimes to those whom he had punished. For my part, I think such a grave charge needs better proof than is forthcoming.

Among the conspirators was one Quintus Curius, a man of good birth but sunk over head and ears in infamy and crime, whom the censors had expelled from the Senate for immoral conduct. As unreliable as he was reckless, he could neither hold his tongue about what he heard nor even keep dark his own misdeeds, being utterly regardless of what he said or did. A woman of good family named Fulvia had long been his mistress; and when he found himself less in favour with her because lack of means compelled him to be less lavish with his presents, he suddenly began to talk big and to promise her the earth – the next moment threatening to stab her unless she complied with his demands. This high and mighty tone was so different from his normal manner that Fulvia insisted on an explanation; and on learning the cause of his arrogant behaviour she decided that such a serious danger to the state must not be concealed. Without mentioning the name of her informant, she told a number of persons the various facts that she had ascertained about Catiline's plot. It was this information, more than anything else, that made people eager to entrust the consulship to Marcus Tullius Cicero. Previously, most of the aristocracy were seething with jealousy, and thought it almost a defilement of the consulship for an outsider, however outstanding his merits, to be elected to it. But when danger threatened, jealousy and pride had to take a back seat.

Accordingly, when the poll took place, Cicero and Gaius Antonius were returned as consuls – which at the time was a bad blow to the conspirators. Yet Catiline's frenzy showed no sign of abating. Every day he enlarged his plans, establishing depots of arms at convenient spots throughout Italy, raising money on his own or his friends' credit and sending it to Fiesole to a man called Manlius, who later on was the first to open hostilities. About this time Catiline is said to have gained many adherents of every condition, including a number of women who in their earlier days had lived extravagantly on money that they obtained by prostituting themselves, and then, when advancing age reduced their incomes without changing their luxurious tastes, had run headlong into debt. These women, he thought, would do good service by acting as agitators among the city slaves and organizing acts of incendiarism; their husbands, too, could be either induced to join his cause, or murdered.

Among their number was Sempronia, a woman who had committed many crimes that showed her to have the reckless daring of a man. Fortune had favoured her abundantly, not only with birth and beauty, but with a good husband and children.* Well educated in Greek and Latin literature, she had greater skill in lyre-playing and dancing than there is any need for a respectable woman to acquire, besides many other accomplishments such as minister to dissipation. There was nothing that she set a smaller value on than seemliness and chastity, and she was as careless of her reputation as she was of her money. Her passions were so ardent that she more often made advances to men than they did to her. Many times already she had broken a solemn promise, repudiated a debt by perjury, and been an accessary to murder. At once self-indulgent and impecunious, she had gone headlong from bad to worse. Yet her abilities were not to be despised. She could write poetry, crack a joke, and converse at will with decorum, tender feeling, or wantonness; she was in fact a woman of ready wit and considerable charm.

* She was the wife of Decimus Junius Brutus, consul in 77 B.C., and mother of the Decimus Brutus who was one of the assassins of Julius Caesar.

CHAPTER III

EARLY STAGES OF THE CONSPIRACY

In spite of the preparations he had made for a *coup d'état*, Catiline was a candidate for the consulship of the following year,* hoping, if elected, to find it easy to use Antonius for his own purposes. Meanwhile he was not idle, but kept on laying all manner of traps for Cicero. The latter did not lack craft or cunning to defend himself. At the very beginning of his consulship he had made many promises, through the agency of Fulvia, to the Quintus Curius mentioned above, and had thereby induced him to betray Catiline's designs. Furthermore, by agreeing to let his colleague Antonius have the governorship of a rich province,† he had prevailed on him to remain loyal; and for his own protection he had secretly organized a bodyguard of friends and retainers.

When the polling-day came and Catiline found that both his candidature and an attempt which he made against the consuls in the Campus Martius had failed,‡ he decided to try extreme measures. Open war was now his only resource, since his secret endeavours had ended in defeat and disgrace. He therefore sent Gaius Manlius to the neighbourhood of Fiesole in Etruria; a certain Septimius, a citizen of Camerino, to Picenum; Gaius Julius to Apulia;§ and others to various

* 62 B.C. † Macedonia.

‡ Elections were held in the Campus Martius beside the Tiber. The election referred to here would normally have taken place in July 63 B.C.; but although Sallust does not mention the fact, we know from Cicero that it was postponed on account of threats uttered by Catiline. The date on which it actually took place is not known. The consuls elected were Decimus Junius Silanus and Lucius Licinius Murena.

§ Etruria is modern Tuscany; Camerino, a town in Umbria; Picenum occupied the southern part of the Marches and the northern part of the Abruzzi; Apulia extended from the promontory of the Gargano to a short distance north-west of Brindisi.

districts where he thought they would be useful. Meanwhile at Rome he had several plans on foot simultaneously, plotting by stealth against the lives of the consuls, organizing acts of arson, and occupying strategic points with armed men. He himself went about armed, and bade his followers do the same, urging them to be continually alert and ready. Day and night he was wide awake and hurrying to and fro, his strength unexhausted by want of sleep or toil. Finally, when all this feverish activity effected nothing, he deputed Marcus Porcius Laeca to summon another meeting of the ringleaders at dead of night.* There, after bitterly complaining of their lack of energy, he informed them that he had sent Manlius on ahead to the fighting force which had been assembled, and others also to begin hostilities at various key points. He himself, he added, was eager to join his army if only he could first destroy Cicero, who was a serious hindrance to his plans. Fear made the rest hesitate; but Gaius Cornelius, a Roman Eques, offered his services and was joined by a senator named Lucius Vargunteius. They decided to go to Cicero's house later that night with a band of armed men and to gain admittance by pretending to make a ceremonial morning call. They would then take him by surprise and assassinate him in his own house before he could defend himself. But Curius, realizing that the consul was in mortal peril, hastened to warn him, through Fulvia, of the trap which was being set for him. Accordingly, the door was shut against them, and they found that they had accomplished nothing by undertaking to commit this atrocious crime.

* The antedating of this meeting at Laeca's house is the most serious of Sallust's mistakes in the *Catiline*. Cicero tells us that it took place on the night of 6 November – i.e. *after* the events described by Sallust in sections 29 (meeting of the Senate at which the 'last decree' was passed on 21 October), 30 (news of Manlius's rising in Etruria on 27 October and the government's preparations for defence); and 31[4] (accusation of Catiline under the *lex Plautia*).

Meanwhile, in Etruria, Manlius was agitating among a populace whose poverty, added to the resentment which they felt at their wrongs, made them eager for revolution; for during Sulla's tyranny they had lost their lands and all the rest of their possessions. He also approached some of the many types of brigands who infested that part of the country, as well as some veteran soldiers from Sulla's 'colonies', whose lavish indulgence of their appetites had exhausted the enormous booty they had brought home.

The news of these events greatly disturbed Cicero, who saw himself beset with difficulties on both sides. The city could no longer be protected from the conspirators by unofficial action on his part; and as to Manlius's army, he had no exact knowledge either of its size or of its commander's intentions. He therefore apprised the Senate of the matter, which had already been a topic of popular gossip. In accordance with its usual practice in serious emergencies, the Senate decreed that the consuls 'should take measures for the defence of the realm', thus conferring upon them the most extensive powers that Roman custom allows it to entrust to magistrates.* This decree authorizes them to levy troops and conduct war, to apply unlimited force to allies and citizens alike, and to exercise supreme command and jurisdiction both at home and abroad. Without it, a resolution of the Popular Assembly is necessary to confer any of these powers upon a consul.

A few days later, a senator called Lucius Saenius read to the House a letter which he said had come to him from Fiesole, stating that Gaius Manlius had taken the field with a large army on 27 October. There were also the usual conflicting rumours. Some reported portents and omens; others had heard that men were being assembled and arms transported here or there, and that at Capua and in Apulia the slaves were rising. Accordingly,

* On this decree, the famous 'last decree of the Senate', see Introduction, p. 168, and Introduction to The Jugurthine War, pp. 23–4.

by decree of the Senate, Quintus Marcius Rex was sent to Fiesole and Quintus Metellus Creticus to the neighbourhood of Apulia. Both these officers were waiting at the gates of Rome, retaining their commands in the hope of a triumph,* of which they were cheated by the quibbling objections of a small clique who made a practice of selling anything, honourable or dishonourable, for a consideration. Of the praetors, Quintus Pompeius Rufus was sent to Capua and Quintus Metellus Celer to Picenum, with instructions to raise forces adequate to deal with the critical situation that had arisen. Rewards were also offered for information about the plot against the state: for a slave, the reward was to be his freedom and a hundred thousand sesterces;† for a free man, double that sum and a pardon for any share he might have had in the conspiracy. Furthermore, the gladiatorial schools were to be broken up and the gladiators sent away to Capua and other towns in numbers proportioned to the resources of each place; and throughout Rome night watches were to be posted by the junior magistrates.

These events had made a profound impression on the people, and had changed the face of the city. In place of the reckless gaiety and pleasure-seeking which a long period of tranquillity had fostered, there was sudden and universal gloom. Everyone was in a state of feverish anxiety; no one thought any place safe or trusted anyone. There was neither open war nor real peace, and each man estimated the danger by the measure of his own dread. The women too, to whom, at the centre of such a great empire, fear of war came as a new experience, beat their breasts, stretched out hands in supplication to heaven, and bewailed the fate of their little

* Quintus Marcius Rex (consul 68 B.C.) had taken part in the war against Mithridates as proconsul in Cilicia (67–66). Quintus Caecilius Metellus Creticus (consul 69) had conquered Crete and organized it as a province (68–66).

† Something like £1,000 at nineteenth-century values.

children; questions were continually upon their lips and terror in their hearts; pride and frivolity were forgotten in the despair with which they anticipated their own and their country's fate.

Catiline's ruthless spirit still pursued its fell design, undeterred by the preparations for defence or by a prosecution which Lucius Paulus brought against him under the law of Plautius.* Finally – either as part of his plan of dissimulation, or with the idea of establishing his innocence if any speaker should denounce him – he attended a meeting of the Senate. Thereupon the consul Cicero, alarmed by Catiline's presence or, it may be, moved by indignation, rendered the state good service by delivering a brilliant oration, which he afterwards wrote down and published.† When Cicero sat down, Catiline began to act his part of complete innocence. With downcast eyes he implored the senators in suppliant tones not to be too hasty in believing anything that was alleged against him. His high birth, he said, and the life he had lived ever since his youth, justified him in entertaining the highest hopes. He was born a patrician; and like his ancestors before him, he had many times been of service to the Roman people. Could it be seriously supposed that such a man stood to gain anything by the ruin of the Republic, when a mere immigrant like Cicero‡ sought to preserve it? He was proceeding to hurl further insults when the whole House shouted him down with cries of 'Enemy!' and 'Traitor!' At this he flew into a towering rage. 'Since I

* This law (*lex Plautia de vi*) had been enacted at some time during the preceding fifteen years, and imposed penalties on anyone convicted of using violence for political ends.

† This is the first of Cicero's four orations against Catiline. It was delivered on 8 November.

‡ A sarcastic reference to the fact that Cicero was a native of Arpinum, a town in the Volscian highlands, betwen sixty and seventy miles south-east of Rome. But as Arpinum had possessed the Roman franchise since 188 B.C., the taunt is not a very effective one.

am encompassed by foes,' he cried, 'and hounded to desperation, I will check the fire that threatens to consume me by pulling everything down about your ears.'*

With these words he dashed out of the Senate House and hurried home, where he pondered deeply on the situation. His murderous plots against the consul were making no headway, and any attempt at arson would be foiled by the patrols. So he thought the best thing to do was to reinforce his army and to employ the time which must elapse before legions could be enrolled in providing everything needful for war. At dead of night, therefore, he set out for Manlius's camp with a few companions, leaving orders for Cethegus, Lentulus, and the most daring and determined of his other accomplices, to do everything possible to increase the strength of their party, to find an early opportunity of assassinating Cicero, and to make arrangements for massacre, fire-raising, and other violent outrages. He himself, he added, would shortly be marching on the city with a large army.

While these events were taking place at Rome, Gaius Manlius sent a deputation of his followers to Marcius Rex with a message to this effect:

'We call gods and men to witness, sir, that our object in taking up arms was not to attack our country or to endanger others, but to protect ourselves from wrong. We are poor needy wretches; the cruel harshness of moneylenders has robbed most of us of our homes, and all of us have lost reputation and fortune. Not one was allowed the benefit of the law established by our ancestors, which should have enabled us, by sacrificing our possessions, to save our persons from

* Here again Cicero shows that Sallust is in error. Sallust introduces the remark as an effective exit-line when Catiline rushed out of the Senate on 8 November. Actually, it was made in July, and was his repartee when he was threatened by Cato with a prosecution. Moreover, Sallust has rather spoiled the point of it. What Catiline said, according to Cicero, was: 'If a fire is raised to consume my fortunes, I will put it out, not with water, but by demolition.'

bondage;* such was the inhumanity of the moneylenders and the praetor.† On many occasions your forefathers took pity on the common people of Rome and issued decrees to relieve their distress. Quite recently, within our own memory, the total of outstanding debts was so huge that all good citizens concurred in permitting them to be discharged in copper instead of silver.‡ Often, too, the commons themselves, either desirous of political power or exasperated by the arrogance of magistrates, took up arms and seceded from the patricians. We, however, are not seeking dominion or riches – the invariable causes of war and quarrelling among human beings – but only freedom, which no true man ever surrenders while he lives. We beseech you and the Senate to rescue your unhappy fellow citizens, to restore to us the legal protection snatched from us by the praetor's injustice, and not force us to seek a means of selling our life's blood as dearly as we can.'

Marcius's reply to this appeal was that if they wished to make any request to the Senate they must lay down their arms and humbly present their petition at Rome; the Roman Senate, he said, had always shown such clemency and compassion that no one ever asked its help in vain.

Catiline, who in the meantime was on his way to join Manlius, wrote to many men of consular rank and other members of the aristocracy, saying that since he had not been able to withstand the group of enemies who persecuted him with trumped-up charges, he was resigning himself to his lot and going to Marseilles as an exile – not because his conscience reproached him with the heinous crime of which he was accused, but in order to preserve the peace of the state and avoid stirring up civil strife by struggling against his fate. A

* Such a law is reputed to have been enacted in the last quarter of the fourth century B.C.

† The *praetor urbanus*, acting as a judge of civil suits.

‡ i.e. a copper *as* was paid in lieu of a silver *sestertius* – a scaling down of debts by 75 per cent.

very different letter was read to the Senate by Quintus Catulus,* who said it had been delivered to him as from Catiline. The following is a copy of it:

'Lucius Catiline to Quintus Catulus. Your very loyal friendship, of which you have given practical proof, and which I value much in the great dangers that confront me, gives me confidence in appealing to your kindness. I do not intend, therefore, to make any formal defence of my new policy. I will however explain my point of view; what I am going to say implies no consciousness of guilt, and on my word of honour, you can accept it as the truth. I was provoked by wrongs and insults and robbed of the fruits of my painstaking industry, and I found myself unable to maintain a position of dignity. So I openly undertook the championship of the oppressed, as I had often done before. It was not that I could not have paid my personal debts by selling some of my estates – and as for the loans raised on the security of others, the generosity of Orestilla would have discharged them with her own resources and those of her daughter. It was because I saw unworthy men promoted to honourable positions, and felt myself treated as an outcast on account of unjust suspicions. That is why I have adopted a course of action, amply justified in my present circumstances, which offers a hope of saving what is left of my honour. I intended to write at greater length; but news has come that they are preparing to use force against me. So for the present I commend Orestilla to you and entrust her to your protection. Shield her from wrong, I beg you in the name of your own children. Farewell.'

Catiline spent a few days with Gaius Flaminius near Arezzo, supplying arms to the local people, whom he had

* Quintus Lutatius Catulus, consul in 78, had long been one of the staunchest supporters of the Senate and the conservative cause. He opposed the grants of exceptional military powers to Pompey in 67 and 66. Below (section 49) we find him trying vainly to induce Cicero to trump up evidence against Caesar of complicity in Catiline's plot.

previously incited to revolt. He then assumed the fasces and other insignia of military command and marched towards Manlius's camp. When this was known at Rome, the Senate declared Catiline and Manlius public enemies, but offered a pardon to the remainder of the rebel forces, except those who stood condemned on capital charges, if they would lay down their arms before a specified date. It was further decreed that the consuls should enrol troops, and that Antonius should hasten with an army in pursuit of Catiline while Cicero guarded the city.

CHAPTER IV

PARTY STRIFE AT ROME

NEVER in its history – it seems to me – had the empire of Rome been in such a miserable plight. From east to west all the world had been vanquished by her armies and obeyed her will; at home there was profound peace and abundance of wealth, which mortal men esteem the chiefest of blessings. Yet there were Roman citizens obstinately determined to destroy both themselves and their country. In spite of two senatorial decrees,* not one man among all the conspirators was induced by the promise of reward to betray their plans, and not one deserted from Catiline's camp. A deadly moral contagion had infected all their minds. And this madness was not confined to those actually implicated in the plot. The whole of the lower orders, impatient for a new régime, looked with favour on Catiline's enterprise.† In this they only did what might have been expected of them. In every country paupers envy respectable citizens and make heroes of unprincipled characters, hating the established order of things and hankering after innovation; discontented with their own lot, they are bent on general upheaval. Turmoil and rebellion bring them carefree profit, since poverty has nothing to lose.

The city populace were especially eager to fling themselves into a revolutionary adventure. There were several reasons for this. To begin with, those who had made themselves conspicuous anywhere by vice and shameless audacity, those who had wasted their substance by disgraceful excesses, and those

* Sections 30[6]; 36[2].

† This surely cannot have been true. Sallust must be exaggerating the popular support for the conspiracy.

whom scandalous or criminal conduct had exiled from their homes – all these had poured into Rome till it was like a sewer. Many, remembering Sulla's victory, and seeing men who had served under him as common soldiers now risen to be senators, or so rich that they lived as luxuriously as kings, began to hope that they too, if they took up arms, might find victory a source of profit. Young men from the country, whose labour on the farms had barely kept them from starvation, had been attracted by the private and public doles available at Rome, and preferred an idle city life to such thankless toil. These, like all the rest, stood to gain by public calamities. It is no wonder, therefore, that these paupers, devoid of moral scruple and incited by ambitious hopes, should have held their country as cheap as they held themselves. Those also to whom Sulla's victory had brought disaster by the proscription of their parents, the confiscation of their property, and the curtailment of their civil rights, looked forward with no less sanguine expectations to what might result from the coming struggle. Moreover, all the factions opposed to the Senate would rather see the state embroiled than accept their own exclusion from political power.

Such was the evil condition by which, after an interval of some years, Rome was once more afflicted. After the restoration of the power of the tribunes in the consulship of Pompey and Crassus,* this very important office was obtained by certain men whose youth intensified their natural aggressiveness. These tribunes began to rouse the mob by inveighing against the Senate, and then inflamed popular passion still further by handing out bribes and promises, whereby they won renown and influence for themselves. They were strenuously opposed by most of the nobility, who posed as defenders of the Senate but were really concerned to maintain their own privileged position. The whole truth – to put it in a word – is

* 70 B.C.; see Introduction, p. 157.

that although all disturbers of the peace in this period put forward specious pretexts, claiming either to be protecting the rights of the people or to be strengthening the authority of the Senate, this was mere pretence: in reality, every one of them was fighting for his personal aggrandizement. Lacking all self-restraint, they stuck at nothing to gain their ends, and both sides made ruthless use of any successes they won.

After Pompey was sent to take command in the wars against the pirates and Mithridates,* the popular party lost ground and the oligarchy became more powerful. They secured a virtual monopoly of public offices, provincial commands, and all other privileges. Living in security and prosperous ease, they had nothing to fear for themselves, and by threats of prosecution they could deter any opponents who were elected to office from rousing the people by violent agitation. But the moment an unsettled situation offered a hope of revolution, the old fighting spirit reanimated the hearts of the popular leaders. If the first engagement had ended in a victory for Catiline, or even in a drawn battle, a terrible catastrophe would certainly have overtaken the state, and the victors would not have been allowed to enjoy their success for long: worn out and enfeebled, they would soon have seen a stronger opponent wrest both power and freedom from their hands.† Even as it was, a number of men who had no part in the plot set out to join Catiline at the start of the campaign. Among them was Fulvius, a senator's son, who was dragged back when already on his way and put to death by his father's command.

* 67–66 B.C.; see Introduction, p. 161.

† By 'a stronger opponent' Sallust means Pompey, who was in Asia Minor at the head of a large army. He had just completed the conquest of Mithridates and was now engaged in reorganizing and extending Rome's eastern provinces.

CHAPTER V

THE BETRAYAL OF THE CONSPIRACY

At Rome, meanwhile, Lentulus was carrying out Catiline's orders. He worked, personally or through agents, on all whose character or fortunes seemed to mark them as fit instruments for revolution, not confining himself to citizens, but approaching all sorts and conditions of men, provided they could be of service in the rising. In pursuance of this policy he directed one Publius Umbrenus to seek out the envoys of the Allobroges* and induce them, if possible, to take part in the war as Catiline's allies. The fact that they were overburdened with public and private debts, as well as the naturally warlike temperament of the Gauls, would, he thought, make it easy to persuade them to such a course. Umbrenus, who had done business in Gaul, was known to many of the leading men in various Gallic communities and knew them personally. So without wasting any time, directly he saw the envoys in the forum, he asked them a few questions about the condition of their country, and then, pretending to be sorry for them, inquired how they hoped to extricate themselves from such serious difficulties. Complaining bitterly about the rapacity of the Roman officials and blaming the Senate for its failure to help them, they said that nothing but death could release them from their misery. 'Why, I myself,' said Umbrenus, 'if only you will act like men, will show you a means of escaping from your misfortunes.' Inspired with high hopes by his words, they implored him to take pity on

* A powerful Gallic tribe whose territory lay between the Rhône, the Isère, and the lake of Geneva, and formed the northernmost part of the Roman province of Transalpine Gaul. Their envoys were in Rome on official business – evidently, as the context shows, to complain of extortion on the part of Roman officials.

them; no task, they declared, could be so formidable or difficult that they would not jump at it, if it would but free their state from debt. He then took them to the house of Decimus Brutus, which was close to the forum, and, thanks to Sempronia, was no stranger to the conspiracy; Brutus was no hindrance, since at the moment he was away from Rome. Umbrenus also summoned Gabinius, in order to give greater weight to the proposal he intended to make, and in his presence told them of Catiline's conspiracy and named his principal accomplices, including among them a miscellaneous collection of entirely innocent persons, with the object of inspiring them with greater confidence. Eventually he received from them a promise of assistance and sent them back to their lodging.

The Allobroges could not for a long time make up their minds what to do. On one side of the scale were their debts, their love of fighting, and the prospect of enrichment if the war was successful. Against these must be set the greater resources of the Roman government and the consideration that, by playing for safety instead of gambling, they could make sure of a reward. In the end the Good Fortune of the Republic prevailed, and they communicated all they had been told to Quintus Fabius Sanga, who regularly acted as their patron in Rome. When Cicero was informed by Sanga of Lentulus's plan, he instructed the envoys to feign great interest in Catiline's conspiracy, and, by getting in touch with the rest of his accomplices and making them fair promises, to try to obtain the clearest possible evidence against them.

At about this time there were disturbances in northern Italy and in Provence, as well as in Picenum, Apulia, and the country of the Bruttii.* The agents whom Catiline had sent to these regions were trying to do everything at once, with a rashness that made it seem almost as though they had lost their reason. By their nocturnal meetings, transportation of

* The toe of Italy.

arms and weapons, and general hurry and bustle, they had caused more alarm than real danger. A number of them had been tried and imprisoned by the praetor Quintus Metellus Celer in accordance with the decree of the Senate, and similar action had been taken by Gaius Murena, the deputy governor of Transalpine Gaul.*

Lentulus and the other conspirators in Rome had now collected what seemed to them a large force, and had decided that as soon as Catiline's army had reached a certain point in its advance towards the city, the tribune Lucius Bestia should convene a public meeting and protest against the steps taken by Cicero, throwing upon that excellent consul the odium of having provoked a conflict which had assumed a very serious character. This was to be the signal for the rank and file of the conspirators to carry out their various tasks during the following night. These, according to report, were distributed as follows. Statilius and Gabinius were in charge of a large body of men who were to start fires simultaneously at twelve chosen spots in the city, in the hope that the ensuing confusion would enable them to obtain access more easily to the consul and the others whose lives they were plotting against. Cethegus was to wait at Cicero's door and make an armed attack upon him, while others did the same to the victims allotted to them. The youths still under age – mostly sons of noble families – were told off to murder their fathers. When the fire and the bloodshed had produced a general panic, they would break out and go to join Catiline. While this was all being decided on and planned, Cethegus kept on complaining that the others lacked spirit and by their hesitance and procrastination were wasting golden opportunities. Action, he said, not debate, was what such a crisis required; he himself was ready to storm the Senate House, if only a few would help

* This province, roughly coextensive with Provence, was acquired about 120 B.C.

him; the rest might stand idle if they pleased. Naturally impetuous and violent, he never hesitated to act, and regarded speed as the first essential for success.

The Allobroges, in accordance with Cicero's instructions, got Gabinius to introduce them to the other conspirators, and demanded from Lentulus, Cethegus, Statilius, and Cassius, a written undertaking for them to carry under seal to their countrymen. Without this, they said it would be difficult to induce them to take such a serious step. All but Cassius unsuspectingly did as they were asked; but Cassius said that he would shortly be going to Gaul in person – and in fact he did start from Rome a short time before the envoys. A man named Titus Volturcius, of Crotone,* was sent by Lentulus with the Allobroges, so that before proceeding to their own country they might confirm their alliance with Catiline by exchanging solemn assurances. Lentulus personally entrusted to him a letter for Catiline, of which the following is a copy:

> Who I am, you will learn from the bearer of this. Reflect what a serious situation you are in, and remember that you are a man. Consider what your interests require. Seek help from all, even from the humblest.

He also sent a message by word of mouth: what, he asked, was Catiline's idea – since he had been declared a public enemy by the Senate – in refusing to enlist slaves? All was ready at Rome according to his orders, and there must be no delay on his part in advancing nearer.

The next step was to fix a night for the departure of the envoys.† Cicero, to whom they had communicated everything, ordered the praetors Lucius Valerius Flaccus and Gaius Pomptinus to wait on the Mulvian bridge‡ for the Allobroges'

* A coastal town on the toe of Italy.

† The night of 2 December.

‡ The Pons Mulvius (now Ponte Milvio or Ponte Molle) carried the Via Flaminia across the Tiber, a little north of the ancient city.

party and to arrest them. He explained the general purpose of their mission but gave them discretion to act as circumstances might require. The praetors, who were experienced soldiers, quietly occupied the bridge, according to their orders, by posting pickets in hiding. When the envoys and Volturcius reached the spot and heard shouting on both sides of them at once, the Gauls quickly realized what the plan was and promptly surrendered to the praetors. Volturcius at first called on the others to resist, and sword in hand defended himself against his numerous assailants. When he saw that the envoys had deserted him, he began by earnestly begging Pomptinus, to whom he was known, to save him, but finally he lost his nerve and yielded to the praetors in as abject fear for his life as if they had been foreign invaders.

When it was all over, a full report was speedily sent to the consul, who, delighted as he was at the news, was at the same time harassed with anxiety. For although he rejoiced in the knowledge that by the discovery of the plot his country was rescued from its peril, yet he had a difficult decision to take. An abominable crime had been brought home to citizens of the highest standing. What was his proper course? To punish them would lay a heavy responsibility on his own shoulders; but to let them go free might mean ruin to the state. So, summoning up his resolution, he sent for Lentulus, Cethegus, Statilius, Gabinius, and also for Caeparius, of Terracina, who was about to set out for Apulia to stir up a revolt among the slaves. They all came without delay except Caeparius, who, having left his house shortly before, had heard of the betrayal of their plans and fled from the city. As Lentulus held the rank of praetor, Cicero himself took him by the hand and conducted him to the temple of Concord, to which he ordered the others to be brought under a guard. The Senate was summoned to meet there,* and before a crowded house

* On 3 December.

Volturcius was led in with the Gallic envoys. The praetor Flaccus had been told to bring a dispatch-box containing the letters which he had obtained from them.

When Volturcius was questioned, first about his journey and the letter he was carrying, and then about his purpose and motive, he began by inventing a story and pretending to know nothing of the conspiracy. Afterwards, on being promised a pardon if he would speak, he revealed all he could of the facts; but he declared that as it was only a few days since he had been called in to help by Gabinius and Caeparius, he knew no more than the envoys: all he could say was that he had often heard Gabinius mention Publius Autronius, Servius Sulla, Lucius Vargunteius, and many others, as being in the plot. The Gauls gave evidence to the same effect, and when Lentulus pretended to know nothing about it they proved his guilt by referring to his letter and by repeating words which he had often used. 'The Sibylline books', he had said, 'prophesied that Rome would be ruled by three Cornelii; Cinna and Sulla had been the first two, and he himself was the third who was destined to be master of the city. Moreover it was the twentieth year since the burning of the Capitol – a year which the soothsayers, when consulted about the meaning of various portents, had repeatedly declared would be marked by civil bloodshed.' The letters were read after each of the accused had acknowledged his own seal, and the Senate then decreed that Lentulus should resign his office and that he and the others should be kept under open arrest. Lentulus therefore was delivered over to Publius Lentulus Spinther, who was then aedile; Cethegus to Quintus Cornificius; Statilius to Gaius Caesar; Gabinius to Marcus Crassus; Caeparius, who had just been caught and brought back, to a senator named Gnaeus Terentius.

The disclosure of the plot produced a *volte-face* in public opinion. The common people, who at first, in their desire for a new régime, had been only too eager for war, now cursed Catiline's scheme and praised Cicero to the skies. If they had been rescued from slavery, they could not have rejoiced more. The other acts of violence that a war would have entailed, far from causing them any loss, would have provided them with plunder; but when it came to incendiarism, this they looked on as something monstrous and inhuman, and particularly disastrous for them, since their sole possessions were their clothes and other articles of everyday use.

On the next day* a certain Lucius Tarquinius was brought before the Senate. He was said to have been on his way to join Catiline when he was arrested and brought back. He offered to give information about the conspiracy if he received a promise of pardon, and on being told by the consul to speak out he made a statement very similar to that of Volturcius, about the preparations for fire-raising and the massacre of loyal citizens, and about the rebels' intended advance on Rome. He went on to say that he had been sent by Marcus Crassus to tell Catiline not to be dismayed by the arrest of Lentulus, Cethegus, and the other conspirators, but to march all the more quickly on that account, with the object both of encouraging those of his partisans who were still at liberty and of facilitating the rescue of the prisoners. The mention of Crassus's name – a nobleman possessed of immense wealth and influence – gave the Senate pause. Some considered Tarquinius's allegation incredible. Others, though they believed it, thought that in such a crisis a powerful man like Crassus should be conciliated rather than provoked. Many, too, were indebted to him as the result of private business transactions. So they all began to shout, saying that the informer was a liar, and demanded a debate on the subject. It was accordingly brought up on the agenda by Cicero, and a full house registered its opinion that the information was false, and decreed that

* 4 December.

Tarquinius should be kept in custody and not permitted to make any further statement unless he revealed the name of the person who had suborned him to fabricate such a grave indictment. Some believed that this charge had been trumped up by Publius Autronius with the object of shielding the other defendants, whose chances of acquittal would be improved if such an influential man as Crassus were incriminated together with them. Another view was that Tarquinius had been set on by Cicero, lest Crassus should make trouble for the government by following his usual practice of coming forward in defence of bad characters. At a later date I actually heard Crassus declare with his own lips that this infamous accusation had been made against him by Cicero.

About the same time Quintus Catulus and Gaius Piso tried in vain by entreaties, cajolery, and bribes to persuade Cicero into putting up the Allobroges, or some other informer, to bear false witness against Caesar. Both these men were bitter enemies of Caesar. Piso, when on trial for extortion, had been denounced by him for unjustly executing a man in northern Italy.* Catulus had hated him ever since they were rival candidates for the chief pontificate;† for at the end of a long career during which he had held the highest offices, he had been defeated by Caesar when the latter was still a comparatively young man. Moreover it seemed an opportune moment to embarrass Caesar, who by his splendid generosity to his friends, and by the lavish scale of his public entertainments when he was in office, had contracted very large debts. On

* This trial took place earlier in 63 B.C. Piso, who governed Cisalpine and Transalpine Gaul in 67–65, was defended by Cicero and acquitted.

† The priests belonging to the College of the *pontifices* were skilled in the elaborate ceremonial of public religious rites, their chief function being to advise the magistrates on matters connected with state cults. The head of the College was the *pontifex maximus*, who, during most of the later Republican period, was elected by a section of the Popular Assembly. The office was one of great respectability and prestige. Caesar had secured election to it (with the aid, it was said, of wholesale bribery) earlier in the year.

finding that they could not prevail upon Cicero to commit this enormity, they took the matter into their own hands. By accosting individuals and circulating falsehoods which they pretended to have heard from Volturcius or the Allobroges, they provoked such intense feeling against Caesar that some Roman Equites who were serving as an armed guard round the temple of Concord – carried away by the gravity of the danger, or by their own excitability – tried to show their patriotism by threatening him with their swords as he came out of the Senate.

CHAPTER VI

THE DEBATE IN THE SENATE AND THE PUNISHMENT OF THE CONSPIRATORS

WHILE the Senate was transacting the business already described, and was voting rewards to the Allobroges and Titus Volturcius for giving information that had been proved correct, Lentulus's freedmen and a few of his dependants were scouring the streets and trying to incite the workmen and slaves to rescue him. Some of them were also seeking the gang-leaders who made a trade of organizing public disturbances. Cethegus, too, sent messages to his slaves and freedmen – a picked and trained body of men – urging them to take the bold step of forming an armed band and breaking into his place of confinement.

On learning of these designs, the consul posted such guards as the emergency required, and after convoking the Senate,* formally consulted it as to what should be done with the prisoners, whom in a full meeting held shortly before this it had already pronounced to be guilty of treasonable conduct. Decimus Junius Silanus† was called on to speak first because he was consul elect. He proposed that the conspirators already in custody, and also Lucius Cassius, Publius Furius, Publius Umbrenus, and Quintus Annius, if they were apprehended, should be executed. (Later in the debate, Silanus was so much impressed by Caesar's speech that he said he would vote for the proposal of Tiberius Nero, which was that the matter should

* On 5 December.

† The second husband of Servilia, a woman very influential among the aristocratic politicians of her day. At one time the mistress of Caesar, by a strange irony she was closely related to one of his bitterest opponents and to the two leaders of the murder plot that destroyed him: for Cato was her half-brother, Marcus Brutus her son, and Cassius her son-in-law.

be adjourned to a later meeting and the guards strengthened in the meantime.) Caesar, when his turn came to be called on by the consul, spoke to the following effect:

'Whoever, gentlemen, is deliberating upon a difficult question ought to clear his mind of hatred and affection and of anger and compassion. It is not easy to discern the truth when one's view is obstructed by such emotions, and all experience proves that those who yield to passion never make politic decisions. If you concentrate your mind on a problem, it can exert its full powers; once let passion come in, it will take control of you and reduce your mind to impotence. There are plenty of examples that I could cite of kings and peoples who have allowed anger or pity to lead them into error. But I would rather mention some cases in which our own ancestors, by controlling their emotions, acted wisely and properly. In the war which Rome fought against King Perseus of Macedon,* the powerful and wealthy state of Rhodes, which our support had made what it was, proved disloyal and turned against us. At the end of the war, when the matter came up for discussion, the Romans feared that if they annexed the island it might be said that they had gone to war to enrich themselves rather than to punish King Perseus for his wrongful conduct; so they let the Rhodians go unpunished.† Similarly, in the whole series of wars with Carthage, in spite of many outrages committed by the Carthaginians in time of peace or during a truce, they never retaliated in kind, even when they had the chance. Such conduct they regarded as unworthy of Romans, even if it might be justifiable as a reprisal. You also, gentlemen, must take care that the guilt of Publius Lentulus and the others does not outweigh your sense of what is fitting, and that you do not indulge your resentment at the expense of your reputation. If a

* In 171–168 B.C.

† Not entirely so: they were deprived of Lycia and Caria, their provinces on the mainland.

punishment can be found that is really adequate to their crimes, I am willing to support a departure from precedent; but if the enormity of their wickedness is such that no one could devise a fitting penalty, then I think we should content ourselves with those provided by the laws.

'Most of the previous speakers have delivered elaborate and impressive speeches in which they deplored the miserable condition of our country. They have dwelt upon the horrors of war and the fate that awaits the vanquished: how girls and boys are ravished, children torn from their parents' arms, wives subjected to the lusts of conquerors, temples and homes pillaged; how amid fire and slaughter, with weapons, corpses, and blood on every side, a cry of universal mourning goes up. But what, in God's name, was the purpose of all this eloquence? Was it to make you detest the conspiracy? As if a man whom the grisly reality has failed to move could be roused by an eloquent speech! That can never be: no mortal man minimizes his own wrongs; many, indeed, resent them more than they ought. But not everyone, gentlemen, is equally free to show his resentment. If humble men, who pass their lives in obscurity, are provoked by anger to do wrong, few know of it, because few know anything about such unimportant people. But men in positions of great power live, as it were, on an eminence, and their actions are known to all the world. The higher our station, the less is our freedom of action. We must avoid partiality and hatred, and above all anger; for what in others would be called merely an outburst of temper, in those who bear rule is called arrogance and cruelty.

'For my own part, gentlemen, I think that any torture would be less than these men's crimes deserve. But most people remember only what happens last: when criminals are brought to justice, they forget their guilt and talk only of their punishment, if it is of unusual severity. I am sure that Decimus Silanus spoke on this serious matter with the best interests of his country at heart, and not from a desire to please anyone or to gratify feelings of personal enmity; for I know him as both a gallant patriot and a man of wise discretion. Yet his proposal strikes me – I will not say, as harsh, for in dealing with such men nothing could properly be described as harsh – but as out of keeping with the traditions of our Republic.

'Surely, Silanus, it must have been either fear or a sense of outrage that impelled you, a consul elect, to suggest a form of punishment that is without precedent. Fear can be left out of the question, especially as, thanks to the precautions taken by our distinguished consul, we have such strong guards under arms. As regards the penalty you proposed, it would be relevant to observe that to men in grief and wretchedness death comes as a release from suffering, not as a punishment to be endured, because it puts an end to all the ills that flesh is heir to, and beyond it there is no place for either tears or rejoicing. But what I want to ask is, Why in heaven's name did you not also propose that the prisoners should be flogged before being executed? Was it because the Porcian law* forbids it? But there are other laws which provide that convicted citizens shall not be put to death, but shall be permitted to go into exile. Was it, then, because flogging is a severer punishment than death? But what penalty can be regarded as harsh or excessive for men found guilty of such a crime? If however it was because you thought flogging a lighter punishment, how can it be logical to respect the law in a comparatively small matter when you have disregarded it in a more important point?

'It may be asked: Who will take exception to any sentence that is passed upon traitors? The lapse of time and the caprice of fortune, which controls the destinies of all men, will one day

* This *lex Porcia*, forbidding the scourging of Roman citizens without allowing an appeal to the people, was proposed, probably in 198 B.C., by the famous censor Marcus Porcius Cato, great-grandfather of the Cato whose speech is recorded in section 52.

produce a change of feeling. These particular men will have richly deserved whatever happens to them. But you, gentlemen, must consider the precedent that you establish for others. All bad precedents originate from measures good in themselves. When power passes into the hands of ignorant or unworthy men, the precedent which you establish by inflicting an extraordinary penalty on guilty men who deserve it will be used against innocent men who do not deserve it. The Spartans, for example, set up in Athens, when they had conquered it, an oligarchy of thirty members.* These men began by executing without trial notorious malefactors whom everyone loathed, and the people rejoiced and said it was well done. After a time they began to act more and more irresponsibly, killing good and bad alike as the whim took them, and intimidating all the rest. Thus Athens was oppressed and enslaved, and paid a heavy price for its foolish rejoicing. In our own times, when the victorious Sulla ordered the execution of Damasippus† and other adventurers whom national calamities had raised to high positions, who did not approve his action? The men were criminals and trouble-makers, whose revolutionary intrigues had harassed the state, and it was agreed that they deserved to die. But those executions were the first step that led to a ghastly calamity. For before long, if anyone coveted a man's mansion or villa – or in the end merely his household plate or wearing-apparel – he found means to have him put on the list of proscribed persons. So those who rejoiced at the death of Damasippus were soon haled off to execution themselves, and the killing did not stop till Sulla had glutted all his followers with riches. I am not afraid that any such action will be taken by Cicero, or in this present age. But in a

* In 404 B.C., at the end of the Peloponnesian war.

† The *cognomen* of Lucius Junius Brutus, praetor 82 B.C.; one of the worst killers among the supporters of Sulla's enemy Marius, he was himself killed by Sulla.

great nation like ours there are many men, with many different characters. It may be that on some future occasion, when another consul has, like him, an armed force at his disposal, some false report will be accepted as true; and when, with this precedent before him, a consul draws the sword in obedience to a senatorial decree, who will there be to restrain him or to stay his hand?

'Our ancestors, gentlemen, never lacked wisdom or courage, and they were never too proud to take over a sound institution from another country. They borrowed most of their armour and weapons from the Samnites, and most of their magisterial insignia from the Etruscans. In short, if they thought anything that an ally or an enemy had was likely to suit them, they enthusiastically adopted it at Rome; for they would rather copy a good thing than be consumed with envy because they had not got it. In this period of imitation they followed the Greek custom of flogging citizens and executing convicted criminals. However, with the growth of the state, and the development of party strife resulting from the increase of population, innocent people were victimized, and other similar abuses grew up. To check them, the Porcian law was enacted, and other laws which allowed condemned persons the alternative of going into exile. This seems to me, gentlemen, a particularly strong argument against our making any innovation. For I cannot but think that there was greater virtue and wisdom in our predecessors, who with such small resources created such a vast empire, than there is in us, who find it as much as we can do to keep what they so nobly won.

'Am I suggesting, you will ask, that the prisoners be released to go and swell Catiline's army? By no means. My advice is that their goods be confiscated, and that they be imprisoned in such towns as are best provided to undertake their custody. Further, that their case shall not thereafter be debated in the Senate or brought before a public assembly; if anyone contravenes this prohibition, the Senate should, I suggest, register its opinion that his action will be treasonable and contrary to the public interest.'

After Caesar's speech most of the other senators contented themselves with a formal expression of agreement with one proposal or the other. But Marcus Porcius Cato, when asked his opinion, spoke to the following effect:

'When I turn, gentlemen, from contemplating the dangerous situation in which we stand to reflect upon the opinions of some of the previous speakers, the impression made on my mind is very different. If I understood them rightly, they were discussing the punishment to be meted out to these men who have planned to make war on their country, parents, altars, and hearths. But the situation warns us rather to take precautions against them than to deliberate what sentence we shall pass on them. Other crimes can be punished when they have been committed; but with a crime like this, unless you take measures to prevent its being committed, it is too late: once it has been done, it is useless to invoke the law. When a city is captured, its defeated inhabitants lose everything.

'I will address myself for a moment to those of you who have always been more concerned for your houses, villas, statues, and pictures, than you have for your country. In heaven's name, men, if you want to keep those cherished possessions, whatever they may be, if you want to have peace and quiet for the enjoyment of your pleasures, wake up while there is still time and lend a hand to defend the Republic. It is not a matter of misappropriated taxes, or wrongs done to subject peoples; it is our liberty and lives that are at stake.

'Many a time, gentlemen, have I spoken at length in this House; many a time have I reproached our fellow citizens for their self-indulgence and greed – and by so doing have made many enemies; for as I had never, in my own conscience, excused myself for any wrongdoing, I found it hard to pardon the sins which other men's passions led them to commit. You took little notice of my remonstrances; but the stability of the state was not impaired by your indifference, because of its great prosperity. Now, however, it is not the question whether our morals are good or bad, nor is it the size and grandeur of the Roman empire that we have to consider. The issue is whether that empire, whatever we may think of it, is going to remain ours, or whether we and it together are to fall into the hands of enemies. In such a crisis does anyone talk to me of clemency and compassion? For a long time now we have ceased to call things by their proper names. To give away other people's property is called generosity; criminal daring goes by the name of courage. That is why our affairs have come to such a pass. However, since such is our standard of morality, let Romans be liberal, if they want to, at the expense of our subjects, let them be merciful to plunderers of the exchequer. But let them not make a present of our life-blood, and by sparing a handful of criminals go the way to destroy all honest men.

'It was an eloquent and polished lecture that Gaius Caesar delivered to you a few minutes ago on the subject of life and death. Evidently he disbelieves the account men give of the next world – how the wicked go a different way from the good, and inhabit a place of horror, fear, and noisome desolation. Therefore he recommended that the property of the accused should be confiscated and that they should be imprisoned in various towns. No doubt he feared that if they remained in Rome, either the adherents of the conspiracy or a hired mob might rescue them by force. What does he think? Are there bad characters and criminals only at Rome, and not all over Italy? Is reckless violence not more likely to succeed where there is less strength to resist it? His proposals are useless if he apprehends danger from the conspirators; and if amid such universal fear he alone is not afraid, I have the more reason to be afraid for myself and for you.* In making your decision about Publius Lentulus and the other prisoners, you must realize that you will also be determining the fate of Catiline's army and of the whole body of conspirators. The more energetically you act, the more will their courage be shaken. Show the slightest weakness, and you will soon have the whole pack of them here barking defiance at you.

'Do not imagine that it was by force of arms that our ancestors transformed a petty state into this great Republic. If it were so, it would now be at the height of its glory, since we have more subjects and citizens, more arms and horses, than they had. It was something quite different that made them great – something that we are entirely lacking in. They were hard workers at home, just rulers abroad; and to the council-chamber they brought untrammelled minds, neither racked by consciousness of guilt nor enslaved by passion. We have lost these virtues. We pile up riches for ourselves while the state is bankrupt. We sing the praises of prosperity – and idle away our lives. Good men or bad – it is all one: all the prizes that merit ought to win are carried off by ambitious intriguers. And no wonder, when each one of you schemes only for himself, when in your private lives you are slaves to pleasure, and here in the Senate House the tools of money or influence. The result is that when an assault is made upon the Republic, there is no one there to defend it.

'I will say no more on that subject. A plot has been hatched by citizens of the highest rank to set fire to their native city. Gauls, the deadliest foes of everything Roman, have been called to arms. The hostile army and its leader are ready to descend upon us. And are you still hesitating and unable to decide how to treat public enemies taken within your walls? I suggest you take pity on them – they are young men led

* A plain hint that Cato believed Caesar to have been privy to Catiline's schemes.

astray by ambition; armed though they are, let them go. But mind what you are doing with your clemency and compassion: if they unsheathe the sword, you may have reason to regret your attitude. Oh yes, you say, the situation is certainly ugly, but you are not afraid of it. On the contrary, you are shaking in your shoes; but you are so indolent and weak that you stand irresolute, each waiting for someone else to act – trusting, doubtless, to the gods, who have often preserved our Republic in times of deadly peril. I tell you that vows and womanish supplications will not secure divine aid; it is by vigilance, action, and wise counsel, that all success is achieved. If you give way to sloth and cowardice, the gods turn a deaf ear to your entreaties: their wrath makes them your enemies.

'In bygone days, during a war with the Gauls, Aulus Manlius Torquatus had his son put to death for fighting the enemy against orders.* That noble youth paid with his life for an excess of valour; and do you, who are trying a set of ruthless traitors to their country, hesitate about the appropriate sentence to pass? If their past lives are urged in extenuation of their crime, by their past lives let them be judged. Spare Lentulus for his high rank – if he ever spared his own chastity and good name, or showed any respect for god or man. Pardon the youth Cethegus – if this is not already the second time he has made war on his country.† As for Gabinius, Statilius, and Caeparius, if they had not been utterly unscrupulous, they would never have plotted as they did against the state.

'To conclude, gentlemen: if we could afford to risk the consequences of making a mistake, I should be quite willing to let experience convince you of your folly, since you scorn

* This statement is incorrect in its details. His *praenomen* was Titus, not Aulus, and it was not in the war which he fought against the Gauls, but in a war against the Latins (340 B.C.), that the incident occurred.

† It is not known what action of Cethegus is here referred to. He may have been concerned in the abortive plot of 66 B.C. (section 18), though none of the authorities mentions him in connexion with it.

advice. But we are completely encircled. Catiline and his army are ready to grip us by the throat, and there are other foes within the walls, in the very heart of our city. We can make no plans or preparations without its being known – an additional reason for acting quickly. This therefore is my recommendation. Whereas by the criminal designs of wicked citizens the Republic has been subjected to serious danger; and whereas, by the testimony of Titus Volturcius and the envoys of the Allobroges, confirmed by the prisoners' own confession, they stand convicted of having planned massacre, arson, and other foul atrocities against their fellow citizens and their country: that, having admitted their criminal intention, they should be put to death as if they had been caught in the actual commission of capital offences, in accordance with ancient custom.'

When Cato sat down, all the senators of consular rank and a large number of others expressed approval of his proposal and praised his courage to the skies, reproaching one another for their faintheartedness. Cato was now regarded as a great and illustrious citizen, and a decree of the Senate was passed in the terms of his resolution.

Reading and hearing much of the glorious exploits of the Roman people in peace and war, on land and sea, I was attracted by the problem of discovering what particular qualities enabled them to carry through such great undertakings. I knew that on many occasions they had only small forces to pit against huge enemy armies, and slender resources with which to do battle against rich and powerful kings; that Fortune had often dealt them cruel blows; and that just as the Greeks were superior to them in eloquence, so the Gauls had formerly outstripped them in martial prowess. After much thought I reached the conclusion that the pre-eminent merit of a few citizens had made all these achievements possible, enabling poor men to conquer rich, a handful to subdue a multitude. But in a later period, when Rome was demoralized by luxury and idleness, the position was reversed: it was now its own greatness that saved the Republic from being ruined by the failings of its generals and magistrates; for many years, as if the vigour of earlier generations were exhausted, there was not one man in Rome of conspicuous merit. In my own time, however, there have been two men of striking worth, though of very different characters – Marcus Cato and Gaius Caesar. Since my subject has brought them to my notice, I do not intend to pass them by in silence, but will give the best description I can of their respective gifts and characters.

In birth, age, and eloquence, they were well matched. They had the same nobility of soul, and equal, though quite different, reputations. Caesar was esteemed for the many kind services he rendered and for his lavish generosity; Cato, for the consistent uprightness of his life. The former was renowned for his humanity and mercy; the latter had earned respect by his strict austerity. Caesar won fame by his readiness to give, to relieve, to pardon; Cato, by never offering presents. The one was a refuge for the unfortunate, and was praised for his good nature; the other was a scourge for the wicked, admired for his firmness. Finally, Caesar had made it a rule to work hard and sleep little; to devote himself to the interests of his friends and to neglect his own; to be ready to give people anything that was worth the giving. For himself he wanted a high command, an army, and a war in some new field where his gifts could shine in all their brightness. Cato's taste was for restraint, propriety, and, above all, austerity. He did not compete in wealth with the wealthy or in party quarrels with the politicians, but with the man of action in deserving, with the virtuous in self-restraint, and with the righteous in strict honesty. He was more concerned to be a good man than to be thought one; and so the less he courted fame, the more did it attend his steps unsought.

When the Senate had adopted Cato's recommendation, the consul thought it best not to wait for nightfall, in case some fresh attempt might be made in the interval, and he therefore directed the triumvirs* to make the necessary preparations for the executions. Posting guards at various points, he personally conducted Lentulus to the prison, while the praetors brought the other prisoners. In the prison is a chamber called the Tullianum, which one reaches after a short ascent to the left. It is about twelve feet below ground, enclosed all round by walls and roofed by a vault of stone. Its filthy condition, darkness, and foul smell give it a loathsome and terrifying air. After Lentulus had been lowered into this chamber, the executioners carried out their orders and strangled him with a noose. So did this patrician, descended from the illustrious family of the Cornelii, a man who had held consular authority at Rome,† meet an end worthy of his character and conduct. Cethegus, Statilius, Gabinius, and Caeparius suffered the same punishment.

* The *tresviri capitales*, who had charge of the prison and performed certain other police duties.

† Lentulus had been consul in 71 B.C. Shortly afterwards he was expelled from the Senate by the censors, but was elected praetor, for a second time, for the year 63.

CHAPTER VII

DEFEAT AND DEATH OF CATILINE

WHILE these events were taking place at Rome, Catiline combined his own contingent of troops with Manlius's original force to form two legions, allotting as many men to each cohort as his numbers permitted. Afterwards, as volunteers or confederates arrived, he drafted them in equal numbers into the cohorts, and soon raised the legions to their full strength, although to begin with he had not had more than two thousand men. But only about a quarter of the whole army was equipped with regulation arms; the rest carried whatever weapons they happened to be able to get – hunting-spears, lances, or even sharpened stakes. On the approach of Antonius's army, Catiline kept to the mountains, moving his encampment now towards Rome, now towards Gaul, and giving his enemy no chance of engaging. He hoped soon to have a large body of troops, if his supporters in Rome succeeded in carrying out their plans. So he refused the help of the slaves who at first flocked to him in large numbers; he was confident that the conspirators could muster enough men, and thought it would be prejudicial to his plans if people saw that he had admitted runaway slaves to a citizens' movement.

However, when news reached the camp that the conspiracy at Rome had been discovered and that Lentulus, Cethegus, and the others mentioned above, had been put to death, the majority of his followers, who had been attracted to the campaign merely by hope of plunder or desire for revolution, dispersed in all directions. The remainder Catiline withdrew by forced marches through rugged mountains to the neighbourhood of Pistoia, intending to escape secretly by side-roads into Gaul. But Quintus Metellus Celer was waiting with three legions in Picenum – since this was precisely the course that he suspected Catiline's difficult position would lead him to adopt. Accordingly, when Metellus learnt from deserters of his enemy's march, he quickly moved off and encamped at the very foot of the mountains which Catiline would have to descend in his hasty retreat to Gaul. Antonius also was not far behind – considering that the size of his army compelled him to keep to comparatively level ground, while the enemy whom he was pursuing were lightly equipped for rapid flight. When Catiline saw that he was shut in between the mountains and the enemy armies, that things at Rome had gone against him, and that he could not hope either to escape or to be relieved, he thought his best course in the circumstances was to try the fortune of war, and decided to engage Antonius as soon as possible. He therefore assembled his troops and addressed them.

'I am well aware, soldiers,' he said, 'that mere words cannot put courage into a man: that a frightened army cannot be rendered brave, or a sluggish one transformed into a keen one, by a speech from its commander. Every man has a certain degree of boldness, either natural or acquired by training; so much, and no more, does he generally show in battle. If a man is stirred neither by the prospect of glory nor by danger, it is a waste of time to exhort him: the fear that is in his heart makes him deaf. However, I have called you together to give you a few words of advice and to tell you the reason for my present purpose.

'You know, I expect, what lack of energy and enterprise Lentulus showed, and how disastrous it has been for himself and for us; and that by waiting for reinforcements to come from Rome I have lost the chance of setting out for Gaul. Our present plight is as obvious to all of you as it is to me. Two enemy armies, one between us and Rome, the other between us and Gaul, bar our way. To remain any longer where we are, however much we might want to, is impossible, because we lack corn and other supplies. Wherever we decide to go, we must use our swords to cut a way through. Therefore I counsel you to be brave and resolute, and when you go into battle to remember that riches, honour, glory, and, what is more, your liberty and the future of your country, lie in your right hands. If we win we shall be sure of getting all we want: we shall have plenty of supplies and all the towns will open their gates. But if fear makes us yield, everything will be against us: no place and no friend will protect a man whom his arms have failed to protect. Moreover, soldiers, our adversaries are not impelled by the same necessity as we are. For us, country, freedom, and life are at stake; they, on the other hand, have no particular interest in fighting to keep an oligarchy in power. Let these thoughts, and the memory of your past valour, inspire you to attack them with all the greater boldness. You might have lived dishonoured lives in exile. Some of you could even have hoped to return to Rome, and – since all your property would have been confiscated – wait for the bounty of others to relieve you. Because such an existence seemed shameful and unbearable for men worthy of the name, you chose the course that has brought you to your present position. If you wish to escape from it, you must act boldly: no one but a victor can survive war to enjoy the fruits of peace. To hope for safety in flight, after turning away from the enemy those arms which are your sole protection, is indeed folly. In battle it is always the greatest cowards who are in the greatest danger; courage is like a wall of defence.

'When I think of you, soldiers, and consider what you have achieved, I have high hopes of victory. Your spirit, youth, and valour give me confidence, not to mention the fact that you are under the necessity of fighting – which makes even timid men brave. The enemy's superior numbers cannot encircle us in such a confined space. But if, in spite of this, Fortune robs your valour of its just reward, see that you do not sell your lives cheaply. Do not be taken and slaughtered like cattle. Fight like men: let bloodshed and mourning be the price that the enemy will have paid for his victory.'

When he had ended his speech, Catiline paused for a little. Then he ordered the trumpet-call for battle to be sounded, formed up his ranks, and led them down to level ground. There, after sending away all the horses – including his own – so that the men might be encouraged by the knowledge that the danger was shared by all alike, he drew up his battle-formation with due regard to the nature of the place and the quality of his troops. A plain was enclosed between mountains on the left and rough rocky ground on the right: here he posted eight cohorts to form the front, and grouped the rest in closer order as a reserve. From these latter he withdrew the centurions, all the picked men and veterans, and the best of the rank and file, and after seeing to it that they were well armed, placed them in the front line. He put Manlius in charge of the right wing and gave the command of the left to an officer from Fiesole. He himself, with his freedmen and some camp-followers, took up his station beside the eagle – one which was supposed to have been carried in Marius's army during the campaign against the Cimbri.*

On the government side, since Antonius was prevented by an attack of gout from taking part in the battle, he entrusted the command to his lieutenant Marcus Petreius, who placed in his front line the cohorts of veterans which he had enrolled to meet the emergency, with the rest of his army behind them as a reserve. Riding up and down, he addressed each soldier by name, encouraging them and bidding them remember that they were fighting against half-armed bandits in defence of their father-

* A German tribe which, with the Teutoni, overran Gaul in the last years of the second century B.C., defeated three Roman armies, and seriously threatened Italy. The Cimbri were defeated in northern Italy by Marius and his colleague Catulus (101 B.C.).

land and their children, their homes and the altars of their gods. He was a good soldier, who for more than thirty years had served with great distinction as military tribune, prefect, lieutenant, and commander; and he knew many of the men personally and remembered their gallant feats of arms. By recalling these he kindled their fighting-spirit.

When he had satisfied himself on every point, he sounded the trumpet-signal and ordered his cohorts to advance slowly, and the enemy's army did the same. As soon as they had come close enough for the light-armed troops to engage, the two armies raised loud shouts and charged together *en masse*. The soldiers threw down their spears and fought with their swords. The veterans, remembering their old-time valour, pressed the enemy vigorously at close quarters. They were bravely withstood, and a struggle of the utmost violence ensued, during which Catiline with his light troops went to and fro in the front line, supporting those who were in difficulties, summoning fresh men to replace the wounded, and attending to everything. Meanwhile he fought hard himself and killed or wounded many of his opponents, performing simultaneously the duties of a hardworking soldier and a good general. Petreius, when he saw Catiline resisting with such unexpected vigour, led the picked men who formed his bodyguard against the enemy's centre, which, thrown into confusion by this attack and able to offer only a sporadic resistance, suffered heavy casualties. Then Petreius made flank attacks on both wings of Catiline's army. Manlius and the officer from Fiesole fell fighting in the front line. Catiline, when he saw his army routed and himself left with a handful of men, remembering his noble birth and the high rank he had once held, plunged into the serried mass of his enemies and fought on till he was pierced through and through.

Only when the battle was over could the daring and ferocity with which Catiline's troops had fought be fully appreciated. Practically every man lay dead on the battle station which he had occupied while he lived. Only some of those in the centre, whom Petreius's bodyguard had dislodged from their position, had fallen a little distance away; and although they had been forced back, they all had their wounds in front. Catiline himself was found far from his own men among the dead bodies of his adversaries. He was still just breathing, and his face retained the look of haughty defiance that had marked him all through his life. Of that whole army which fought and fled, not a single free-born citizen was taken prisoner: all were as careless of their own as of their enemies' lives. The victory of the government forces, however, was not gained without blood and tears: all the best fighters had either been killed in the action or come out of it badly wounded. Many who came from the camp to view the battle-field or to loot, as they went about turning over the rebels' corpses, found friends, relatives, or men who had been their guests or their hosts. Some also recognized the face of an enemy. Thus diverse feelings affected all the army: gladness and rejoicing were tempered by grief and lamentation.

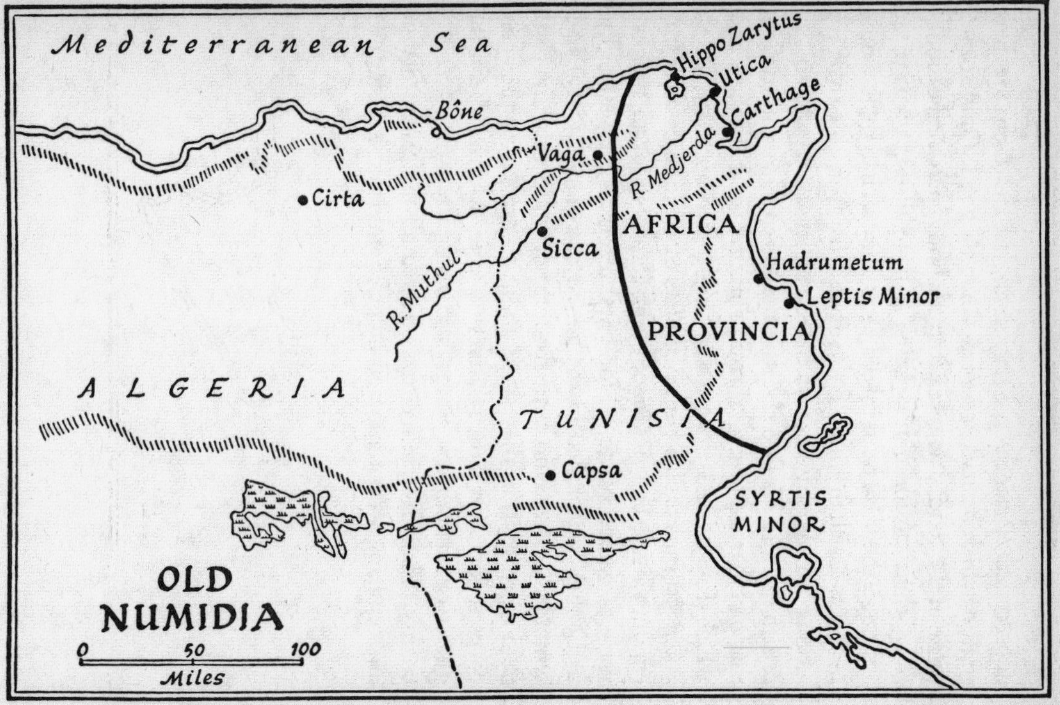
Mediterranean Sea
Hippo Zarytus
Utica
Carthage
Bône
Vaga
R. Medjerda
Cirta
AFRICA
Sicca
R. Muthul
Hadrumetum
Leptis Minor
PROVINCIA
ALGERIA
TUNISIA
Capsa
SYRTIS MINOR
OLD NUMIDIA
0
50
100
Miles

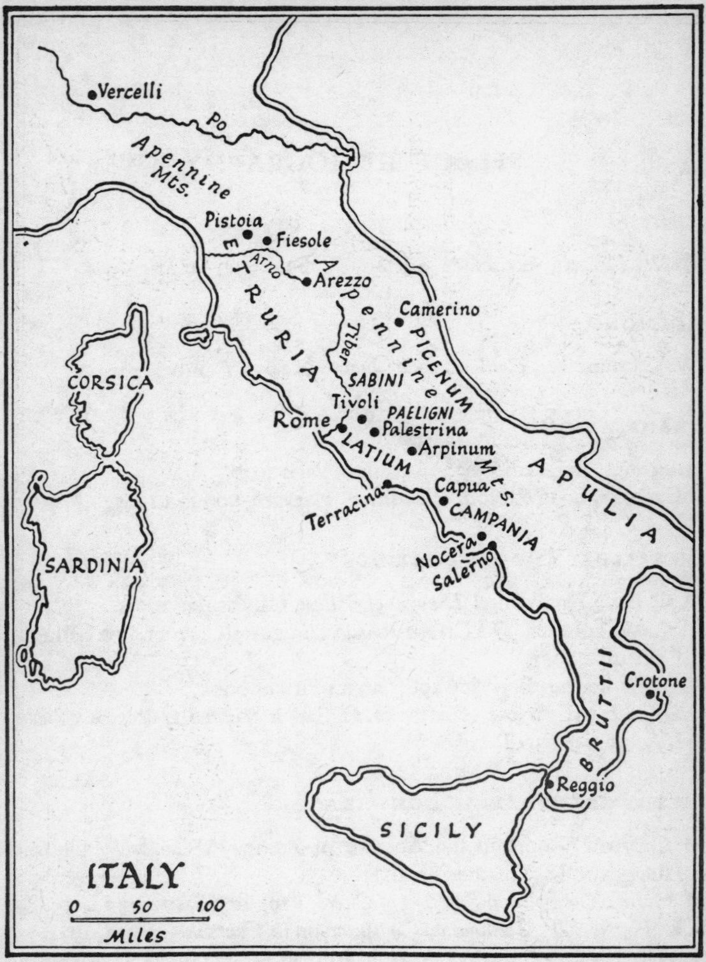
Vercelli
Po
Apennine Mts.
Pistoia
Fiesole
Arno
Arezzo
ETRURIA
Apennine Mts.
Camerino
Tiber
PICENUM
SABINI
Tivoli
PAELIGNI
Rome
Palestrina
LATIUM
Arpinum
APULIA
Capua
Terracina
CAMPANIA
Nocera
Salerno
CORSICA
SARDINIA
BRUTTII
Crotone
Reggio
SICILY
ITALY
0 50 100
Miles

SELECT BIBLIOGRAPHY

TEXT

A. W. Ahlberg, revised A. Kurfess, Teubner text, Leipzig 1954.

EDITIONS

W. C. Summers, *Catiline*, 1900; *Jugurtha*, 1902, Cambridge.

TRANSLATIONS

A. Ernout, Bude edition, 2nd edition, Paris 1946.
J. C. Rolfe, Loeb edition, 6th edition, Harvard-London 1965.

ON SALLUST AND HIS WRITINGS

D. C. Earl, *The Political Thought of Sallust*, Cambridge 1961.
M. L. W. Laistner, *The Greater Roman Historians* (Chapter 3 on Sallust), California 1947.
R. Syme, *Sallust*, Berkeley 1964: an important book.
See also the review of it by D. C. Earl in *Journal of Roman Studies* LV, 1965, p. 232 ff.

ON THE CATILINARIAN CONSPIRACY

M. Cary on 'Rome in the Absence of Pompey', *Cambridge Ancient History* vol. IX, Chapter 11, 1932.
M. Grant, *The Political Speeches of Cicero*, Penguin Classics 1969.
E. G. Hardy, *The Catilinarian Conspiracy in its Context*, Oxford, 1924.
A. N. Sherwin-White, 'Violence in Roman Politics', *Journal of Roman Studies* XLVI, 1956.

ON THE JUGURTHINE WAR

H. Last on 'The Wars of the Age of Marius', *Cambridge Ancient History*, vol. IX, Chapter 3, 1932.
M. Holroyd in *Journal of Roman Studies* XVIII, 1928.

INDEX

(The references are to pages)

INDEX